India
The Challenge
of Change

James Traub

India

The Challenge of Change

JULIAN MESSNER NEW YORK

Copyright © 1981, 1985 by James S. Traub

All rights reserved
including the right of reproduction
in whole or in part in any form.
Published by Julian Messner,
A Division of Simon & Schuster, Inc.
Simon & Schuster Building
Rockefeller Center
1230 Avenue of the Americas
New York, New York 10020

JULIAN MESSNER and colophon are
trademarks of Simon & Schuster, Inc.

Manufactured in the United States of America

Library of Congress Cataloguing in Publication Data

Traub, James.
    India, the challenge of change.

    Includes index.
    Summary: A description of modern India and its
development, including chapters on daily life, religion,
government, agriculture and industry, and foreign
relations.
    1. India—Juvenile literature. [1. India] I. Title.
DS407.T7   1985   954   85-8884
ISBN 0-671-60460-0

10 9 8 7 6 5 4 3 2

Contents

India
The Challenge
of Change

1
The Continental Nation

If you could gain a high enough vantage point to take in all of India at once, you would be astonished to realize that the immense sprawl of languages, customs, religions, and physical and geographical features belong to a single country. Only a continent could house so much variety, so many contradictions. As a single nation India seems downright improbable; but it has been one since it gained independence from the British in 1947. During the 3,500 years before that date India resembled a vast checkerboard of princes and peoples and warring territories. Independence has given all Indians a common destiny, but one can scarcely imagine India ever attaining the uniformity of any European nation or even of the United States.

At its northernmost summit India reaches into the arid Tibetan plateau. The tiny hamlet of Leh, 60 miles from the Chinese border in eastern Kashmir, huddles against the hills of a windy tundra 11,000 feet above sea level. Ancient

Buddhist monasteries ring the town, and others are hidden
so deep in the barren cliffs and mountains that when the
marauding Genghis Khan swept westward from Mongolia
almost nine hundred years ago, he passed by without spot-
ting them.

Scarcely 150 miles to the west, India seems to be transformed into Switzerland. Western Kashmir is a long, grassy
meadow, dusted with wild flowers and dotted with lakes; the
massive Himalayas, rising to 25,000 feet, serve as a backdrop
to every scene. Shepherds, wearing long coats to their knees
and shoes knitted from wool, tend their flocks thousands of
feet above the cities and towns and live in wooden lean-tos
built against the hillsides.

But though the Himalayas serve as the sacred abode of the
Hindu gods and the source of the holy rivers, most Indians
will never see a great mountain, or a natural lake, or an
ocean, or even a large forest. For much of India is plains:
endless horizons with a few scattered trees and occasionally
a mud hut, slow undulations with perhaps a water hole and a
wallowing buffalo; green from the summer monsoon through
October or November, slowly withering thereafter (it will
rain a few times until the middle of the next June) to a
parched surface almost painful to look at during a lengthy
train ride.

The variety remains. Punjabis, in the north at the foot of
the hills, are tall, beefy, and businesslike. Their well-tended
and well-irrigated fields of wheat turn the state into a sea of
gold in April and permit the owners to build solid brick
homes, buy television sets—an antenna on a farmer's home
was an unimaginable sight until recently—and send their
children to study abroad. New Delhi, the nation's capital,
sits at the southern edge of Punjab and has Punjabi cab
drivers and Punjabi food. But this elegant and prosperous
city boasts broad avenues, fountains, and gardens green

even in the driest months, meticulously swept red clay sidewalks, rambling colonial homes with neat lawns. Land in central New Delhi sells for $50,000 an acre and up.

To the south and west of Delhi stretches the desert state of Rajasthan, one of the most barren and infertile states of India. Yet, perhaps to compensate for their lifeless environment, the women of Rajasthan dress in resplendent skirts of tropical reds and greens. India's most extravagant maharajahs built gorgeous palaces that still rise from Rajasthan's bare earth.

The forests of Madhya Pradesh, Rajasthan's southeastern neighbor, preserve a way of life that predates the arrival of the Aryan culture 3,500 years ago. The tribes of Madhya Pradesh—tribal peoples are scattered throughout India— still hunt with bow and arrow, disdain agriculture, and preserve such ancient institutions as the youth dormitory, a coeducational school where young people learn basic skills, native lore, and, entirely free from the intervention of elders, the facts of life.

In Bihar, yet farther to the east, landlords still hold entire villages in subjection, as they have since the British handed over vast tracts of land to them in the late eighteenth century. The largest landowners control 10,000 acres or more— in a state where the average holding does not reach two acres—patrol their territory with private, gun-wielding armies, bribe and terrorize local officials, and keep the landless peasants and tenants who work for them in a state not far from bondage.

The southern states, meanwhile, have remained almost aloof from the waves of invasion that have crossed northern India over four millennia. Although the north Indian languages descended, like English, from the Indo-European language group, the four principal southern tongues have a wholly different origin; that is, English has more in common

with the speech of Delhi than do the languages spoken only 1,000 miles away.

Southern urbanites thus speak English with an accent completely different from northerners'. Southerners worship different gods, and are more likely than northerners to abstain, for religious reasons, from alcohol and meat. Southerners have narrow, bony faces; northerners are broader and more plump. Southerners wear *lungis*, or skirts; northerners

The mountaintop town of Leh, perched atop the barren cliffs of Ladakh (Photo courtesy of Air India)

wear pajama pants or trousers. Northerners wear shirts; southerners, unless they have white-collar jobs, often go bare-chested.

Kerala, India's southwesternmost state, looks like nothing else in the country. Kerala's interior is dense jungle, green and dripping even in May, thick with palms and bananas and four-foot-high jackfruit and trees that yield delicate wood, and higher up in the hills, vast tea plantations, the closely

5

packed tea bushes leveled as smooth as a lawn. And in this most colorful of all states, the women wear white saris, the wrap-around garments common in India.

India has fourteen languages printed on its currency (the rupee, worth about eight cents). English is the most commonly used language for scientific and commercial purposes. Hindi is the official language, though it is understood by only a large minority of the nation. Southerners will not have Hindi imposed on them, thus making a national language

A waterway in the green, tropical interior of Kerala, lush even in the midst of the dry season (Photo courtesy of Government of India Tourist Board)

impossible. India has two major religions—Hinduism, which is practiced by 70 percent of the population, and Islam, to which another 20 percent adhere. India also has sizable numbers of Sikhs, Buddhists, Parsis, Jains, and Christians. And Hinduism itself is further divided into literally thousands of castes, separating shoemakers from laundrymen, farm laborers from landowners, assigning each of them a definite status in a myriad order, and accentuating the differences that already divide them from one another.

And one can no more speak of "Indian culture" than of
"Indian religion" or "Indian language." While all major
European countries, and the United States as well, share the
common form of classical dance known as ballet, each region
in India has its own classical dance form, as well as innumerable varieties of popular dance. In Kathak dance, which
originated in the southwest, the dancers wear layers of ankle
bracelets, and, by taking a step for each of the rapid drum-
beat notes, play out the accompanying music with their feet.
Bharata natyam, which many think of as India's greatest
dance form, demands that the dancer use specific facial ex-
pressions as well as exact positions of the arms, hands,
fingers, hips, knees, and feet in enacting a complex tale,
often a love story of the gods. In all forms of Indian dance the
dancer maintains a perfect composure even in the midst of
the wildest movement.

Indian classical music, which has become familiar in the
United States, differs less from region to region than does
dance. Some of the melodies are as much as 2,000 years old,
as are the steps and the tales involved in dance. The most
common lead instruments are the sitar in the north and the
vina in the south, both of which resemble the guitar but
produce a more resonant, reverberating sound. The playing
is improvisational, as in jazz: the lead player announces the
melody he has chosen—one appropriate to the dawn or the
evening, cheerful or melancholy—and slowly begins to ex-
plore it. Later he is joined by a drummer playing one of
several kinds of drum to add rhythm. In the south, a violinist
may be added to the group. The piece may go on for any
amount of time—at weddings a sitarist may play all night—
with the pace normally growing faster and faster, the two
players almost challenging each other to keep up, until they
finish in perfect unison, like a pair of dancers whirling to a
perfectly balanced stop.

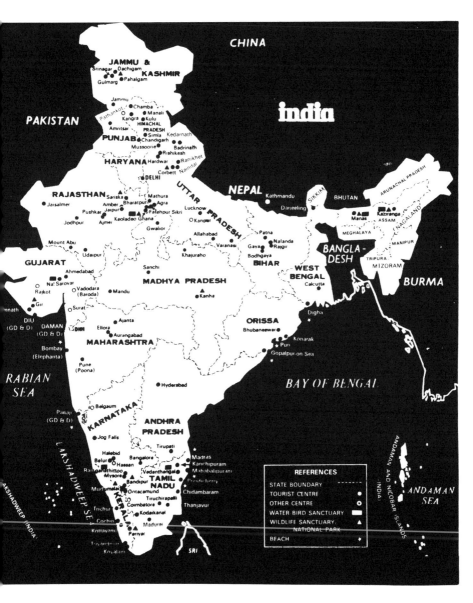

Despite the gulf that separates northerner from southerner, Hindu from Muslim, upper caste from lower caste—distinctions that have led, in each case, to scenes of butchery and riot—Indians are not as alien to one another as Italians are to Germans, or Mexicans to Swedes. India is one nation, not only politically but in some deeper sense. Some 80 percent of the population live in villages of a thousand dwellers or so; most residents of towns and cities are only a generation removed from their village origins. The stoniness of the

Marine Drive in Bombay, India's most cosmopolitan city (Photo courtesy of Government of India Tourist Board)

earth, the fickleness of the weather, the difficulty of finding a suitable mate for a marriageable daughter, anxiety over a sign of sickness in the cattle—these are the daily concerns of the vast majority of Indians. And similar experience, over countless generations, naturally breeds a certain likeness of personality and instinct. Although it is difficult to generalize about 700 million people, it is safe to say that Indians by and large are an essentially conservative people, strongly bound to tradition, suspicious of change. In their powerful ties to

family, religion, caste, and community, Indians are almost
the opposite of Americans, who pride themselves on adven-
turousness, on "traveling light." On the one hand, Indians
are often said to be fatalistic, in that suffering comes as no
surprise to them; they also, on the other hand, accept their
deprivation with great dignity. A calm seems to pervade
even the most hectic or dire scenes in India; a calm born not
only of resignation but of devotion to a long, uninterrupted
tradition.

Even India's divisions serve to bind its people together.
The caste system, which non-Hindus do not accept but can
hardly escape, includes everyone in a single grand scheme
and assigns each individual a place in society. A washerman
knows that he is superior to a tanner, equal to another
washerman, inferior to a shopkeeper. He has obligations to
each and expectations of each. Nirad Chaudhuri, an Indian
but a severe critic of his society, has described caste as "a
social organization that contributes to order, stability, and a
regulation of competition."

The caste system has been in operation for more than
three thousand years, though not without change. The simple building blocks of Indian life—family, religion, custom—
have changed slowly and gradually in that time. India has
been subjected to one invasion after another, but so deep-
rooted are its habits that it changes the intruder rather than
itself. The United States, conversely, hasn't been menaced
by outsiders for a century and a half, yet with its own racing
engine it seems to produce a revolution every generation—
in beliefs, in social relations, even in personality. Many people in industrialized nations feel a need to slow down, to
stave off more "future shock," to preserve the lessons and
habits of the past. Developing countries, India among them,
seem to suffer from the opposite problem. They must goad
themselves out of age-old patterns, convince a conservative

people that change is in its interest, while clinging at the same time to the essential values that have given people a sense of purpose. And this has begun to happen. Over the last several decades the average Indian has changed in fundamental ways. The word "progress" can be heard from the most uneducated peasant, though he may fear that progress is for others, not himself.

India seems to have changed little, but its values, its customs, and its institutions didn't just happen by accident; they were built bit by bit. We cannot claim to understand the United States unless we have studied the people who came here and what happened to them once they arrived. The same applies even more to India, which has had so much more time—ten times more—to build the culture we see today.

2

The Pattern of the Past

1 The Aryan March

Five thousand years ago, when the peoples of Europe were hauling stones across the face of the continent and grubbing out a meager existence, Indians throughout what is now western and southern Pakistan and Punjab, and even farther to the east, were living in elaborately designed cities, with sturdy houses, broad, straight roads, public baths, and drainage systems that were hardly equaled until the Roman era three thousand years later. Archaeologists refer to this sophisticated culture as the Indus Valley civilization and regard it as the eastern wing of the great culture that flourished at the same time in Mesopotamia and across Persia.

The Indus Valley cities, their populations as great as 35,000, traded extensively with their western neighbors and ate fish brought from the Arabian sea. They were manufacturing cotton into textiles two thousand years before the process was known to the West. Early invaders were astonished to find the natives "taking their wool from the earth."

Identical principles of design and construction were used in cities separated by hundreds of miles, and perhaps by several centuries. In other words, the Indus Valley culture was not only so thoroughly established as to be the same in one place as another, but also too conservative to change rapidly; five thousand years later, Indian society seems to have kept the same habits of conservativeness and gradual change.

But five thousand years ago, according to archaeologist John Marshall, the Indus Valley civilization was "already age-old and stereotyped on Indian soil, with many millennia of human endeavour behind it." Usually we think of Mesopotamia as the cradle of civilization, but evidence suggests that the society of northwestern India and Pakistan, which has preserved its essential spirit over countless generations, deserves equal billing.

As the great cities of the Indus grew old and rich, a new people, adventurous and militant, began a slow migration southward from the harsh climate of northeastern Europe— lands that are now East Germany and Poland. These were the Aryans, destined to dominate Europe, Turkey, Persia, and, finally, India. The Aryans migrated in three branches. The westward movement created the peoples now called Greeks, Latins, Celts, and Teutons—that is, Europeans. The southern thrust led to the culture known in the Old Testament as Hittite. And the eastern migration carried these indomitable tribes across the great steppes of central Asia.

Conquering most of Middle Eastern civilization along the way, the tribes finally settled in Persia—what is now Iran— and remained there for several centuries. But restlessness, or possibly a dispute of some kind, set the Aryans moving eastward once more. Pouring through the mountain passes of Afghanistan and then turning southward—the route that was to be taken by innumerable conquerors until the British changed the rules by traveling across the ocean—the Aryans wiped out the cities of northwestern India, starting in about 1750 B.C. With neither military preparedness nor adequate weapons, for they were a commercial rather than a warlike people, the natives were no match for the Aryans, who fought on Persian horses, and, apparently, in chariots.

II The Aryan Settlement

One way of understanding the baffling era of ancient Indian history—the period stretching from the Aryan settlement to roughly A.D. 1000—is to follow what seem to be the two most important developments of the period: the struggle of tribes and rulers with one another to gain a foothold, expand a kingdom, and, finally, bring the entire continent under submission; and the gradual unification of this politically chaotic nation under one religion, with its own unique social order.

The Aryans were the pilgrims who spread what we now call Hinduism throughout the continent, though they left political power in the hands of various warring tribes. Little is known about the thousand years that followed the initial Aryan invasion, in part because this new people practiced farming and herding rather than city-building and trade; they left few monuments behind and had no writing. Their restless migration continued eastward until they reached the banks of the Ganges. From there, over a period of centuries, they drifted southward, mingling with the indigenous peoples rather than seeking to exterminate them, always imparting the religion that they were evolving in the midst of their slow migration. Within a thousand years or so they had colonized the entire continent, a trick not repeated for another five hundred years. The journey of the Aryans finally ended 1,500 years later and perhaps 8,000 miles from where it had begun, but they had given to their final home a common religion, which they called Vedanta; a language, which was known as Sanskrit; and the means of organizing the unruly society, which we call the caste system.

Modern-day Hindus have no single holy book, but their most venerable texts are the four Vedas composed by the Aryans during their wandering. The most ancient of them, the *Rig-Veda*, was two thousand years old before it was written down; the Vedas were authoritatively collected in the middle of the first millennium before Christ, but, despite the availability of writing, they were preserved in the priests' memories—thousands upon thousands of verses for yet another millennium.

Vedanta, the religion of the ancients, means "the end of the Vedas" and is based on the later Vedas, as well as the Upanishads and the Brahmanas, which followed soon thereafter. These holy books contain two essential precepts so far as the average person—the worker rather than the philosopher—is concerned, and modern Hindus take them as seriously as did their ancestors. They are the laws of *dharma* and *karma*. Dharma is the law of duty; it says that a man must do what is right for a person in his position. A warrior must fight; a priest impart holy wisdom, and neither bear arms nor engage in work. A laborer or tradesman must obey priest and king. All must abide by the tortuously complex web of social obligations that had already developed by the end of the Vedic period. The Vedanta also required, more vaguely, obedience to a universal dharma of friendship, generosity, and the like. Karma is not a moral law but a natural one. It tells the worshipers that their every act in life will have some consequence in the next life. Good Hindus—those who abide by their dharma—will return higher up on the social scale. Great ones may return as god figures or may even be relieved of the endless round of birth, death, and rebirth into the world of pain and illusion; bad Hindus may come back as animals or even as plants.

The caste system, which we will discuss in greater detail later on, and the laws of dharma and karma support one another perfectly. By the time of their arrival in India the Aryans had already created permanent classes of priests, known as *Brahmans*, and warriors, called *Kshatriyas*. A third class, the merchants, or *Vaishyas*, probably also came from their own ranks at first. The people they found there, whom the Vedas refer to as *dasas*, or slaves, were absorbed into the system as *Sudras*, who were further subdivided into "pure" and "impure," with the latter effectively exiled from the caste system and now called "Untouchables."

The law of dharma thus kept all people in their places, ensuring that the caste rules were thought of as the ultimate, holy rules. And karma provided a moral explanation for each one's position in the social scale—Brahmans were believed to have led more virtuous past lives than Sudras—and gave an incentive for satisfying one's dharma in the here and now. It should come as no surprise that it was the Brahmans who developed this tidy system. Over the centuries they were able to build up tremendous wealth and almost divine status without much complaint from the lower castes; and, being the only ones who were familiar with the holy books, the Brahmans were free to interpret them as they wished—and, to some extent, they still are.

III *The Great Empires and the Rise of New Religions*

Political organization developed slowly during the period of the Aryan settlement. The first great Aryan empire sprang up near the fertile Ganges, in present-day Bihar. The Magadhan dynasty rose in the seventh and sixth centuries before Christ and had already developed a flourishing urban culture by the time of the birth of ancient India's two great prophets, Buddha and Mahavira, the founder of Jainism. This development proved fortunate for both the prophets and the ruler.

Warring with other tribal groups, the Magadha brought much of northern India beneath its dominance. Operations were interrupted, however, by the arrival of Alexander the Great, fresh from conquering most of the known world. Alexander swept across northwestern India between 327 and 324 B.C., reducing the local kingdoms to a shambles, often after stiff opposition. Unwilling to remain and absorb his gains into his empire, Alexander withdrew, leaving a remnant of his army. Suddenly northern India was up for grabs. Chandragupta, a Maurya (his family name) by birth, usurped the Magadha throne, proceeded to muster an army of 600,000 and, in a quarter of a century, brought all of northern India, including much of Pakistan and eastern Afghanistan, under his control, and then extended his rule southward and westward. No one before Chandragupta, and no one for many centuries afterward, conquered such a sizable portion of the continent.

Chandragupta's son, Bindusara, ruled for an additional twenty-five years and was succeeded by Asoka, a king of whom H. G. Wells said, "More men living cherish his memory today than have ever heard the names of Constantine and Charlemagne." When Asoka ascended the throne, probably in 274 B.C., the Kalingas were the only powerful tribe independent of the Mauryas. The Kalingas ruled what is now Andhra Pradesh. Asoka waged war against them and emerged victorious from the sort of bloodbath typical of the time: 100,000 soldiers were killed and 150,000 captured, while many times that number of civilians died. Asoka was horrified at the carnage. Returning to his capital of Pataliputra (now Patna), he renounced warfare and killing and proclaimed his conversion to the nonviolent religion, Buddhism, then flourishing in the Magadhan region. Asoka began by reforming the royal household. Vast herds had been slaughtered daily to feed the court; Asoka first reduced the figure to two pheasants and a deer and then abolished meat altogether. He forbade his subjects to kill a wide variety of animals. And never again did Asoka take to the battlefield, even though a single brief foray into the South would have made him emperor of all India.

Asoka revolutionized the very idea of kingship: he sought greatness in bringing virtue and happiness to his people rather than in enrolling them in his conquests. Naturally he used his great authority to keep his kingdom together, and some evidence exists that he employed an extensive network of spies. But Asoka's principal concern was to spread Buddhism and its code of ethical conduct throughout his dominions and throughout the world. He sent religious emissaries, not armies, to Kashmir and Sri Lanka, to the Middle East, and to west and southeast Asia. His edicts, inscribed on rocks across India, counseled obedience to elders and Brahmans (a word he used to mean all wise men), honesty, charity, justice, and kindness to travelers, for whom he built rest houses along the road. The vegetarianism now common in India, as well as the abstention from liquor, originated with Asoka. Despite his passionate adherence to Buddhism, he embraced religious tolerance, proclaiming, "All sects deserve reverence for one reason or another."

Asoka's concern for the welfare of his citizens made him a tireless administrator, given to building great public works and ruling conscientiously over his system of governors, commissioners, inspectors, and revenue officials. "At all times and at all places . . . the official reporter should keep me informed of the people's business. . . . At any hour and at any place, work I must for the commonweal."

No ancient king contributed more to modern India than Asoka: the emphasis on nonviolence and vegetarianism, the very idea of benevolent kingship, and, above all, the transformation of Buddhism from an exclusive intellectual sect to a popular and ultimately international religion. Nevertheless, Asoka's pacifism probably accelerated the decline of his kingdom. Within half a century after Asoka's death in 232 B.C., a reduced version of the Maurya empire had been usurped by a smaller rival—an extraordinarily rapid decline for India's first continental power.

Northern India, after the Mauryas, reeled beneath one foreign attack after another. The Greeks and then the Bactrians, or Indo-Greeks, continued to attack northwestern India through the first century after Christ. One of them, Menander, converted to Buddhism and remains a heroic figure in Indian Buddhism under the name King Milinda. The Bactrians were succeeded by the Kushan dynasty, from Mongolian China. Establishing their capital at Peshawar, in northwestern Pakistan, they stretched their empire to the Ganges before they were driven from India in the third century. The Huns, or Hunas, arrived in the north somewhat tentatively in the fourth century and then swept over the decaying empire of the Guptas, ancient India's greatest dynasty after the Mauryas, during the next century. Each invader was eventually driven out by a local dynasty, but no Indian groups, save the Guptas, were able to extend their empire across most of the north.

While threats from abroad undermined the possibility of a united India, challenges from within began to menace the dominance of the deeply entrenched Hindu order. By the time of the birth of Mahavira and Buddha, in the seventh and sixth centuries before Christ, the Vedas were already a thousand years old, the great migration was finished, and Vedanta had lost much of its experimental fervor and youthful vigor. The Brahmans had become wealthy autocrats. They performed no labor but benefited from land grants and tax revenues and owned much cattle and jewelry. The caste system was beginning to lose its flexibility. The simple rules of dharma and karma had vanished beneath a welter of metaphysical speculation and magic. Religions that stray from their source often suffer the rod of correction. So it was with the Hebrews and Christ, the Catholic Church and Luther, and Vedanta and Mahavira and Buddha.

Mahavira's challenge dissipated rapidly. Born a Kshatriya, he rejected the priesthood and its rituals and denied the existence of God. Jainism, the stern faith that he founded, required asceticism as the sole path to salvation and demanded absolute nonviolence. A proper Jain ought not even light a lamp at night lest he burn a moth. Jainism attracted disgruntled urbanites from Magadha but proved too austere to attract a mass following. When the Jains turned to trading and money-lending several centuries later they were absorbed into the Hindu order as a new caste, and today Jains, save for a small number of monks, remain firmly within the caste order.

Buddha, like Mahavira, came from noble stock (he was born a Kshatriya in 545 B.C.) and attacked the rituals and religious prerogatives of the priesthood. Buddha, too, had no use for the new speculations and magic rituals of the Brahmans. He would neither affirm nor deny the existence of God or of any ultimate principle or of any claim of wisdom that could not be explained logically; he prescribed no prayers and described no visions of heaven or hell. Instead Buddha offered release from the world that his experience saw: "Birth is suffering, old age is suffering, death is suffering, to be united with what one loves not is suffering, to be separated from what one loves is suffering." If at the end of every desire stands nothing more than pain, the only solution is utter detachment, to "wander lonely as the rhinoceros," as Buddha said. Naturally those who understand the universality of suffering will be compassionate and generous and tolerant, but they will permit none of these moral impulses to become strong emotions, which would only attach them all over again to the world of pain.

Buddhism, as we know, proved a great deal more successful than Jainism. After Buddha's death a reform movement, known as Mahayana, gained popularity throughout India, especially during the reign of Asoka. The orthodox faith had attracted the same class as Jainism: intellectuals, urbanites fed up with Brahman domination, lower-caste adherents attracted by a more democratic sect. Mahayana supplied much that Buddha had expressly rejected but that the masses of people naturally enjoyed: saintly figures called *bodhisattvas*, with whom the believer could feel a more personal relation; the transformation of Buddha into more or less of a god; and permission to paint and sculpt human figures. This led to the romantic, sentimental cave art that has survived to this day.

As Mahayana grew in popularity it began to resemble Vedanta. A complex philosophy replaced Buddha's simple directives. Great universities investigated the knowledge of the day. To the bodhisattvas were added ever more deities, many of them borrowed from the rival faith. Magic entered the religion in various forms. And the popularity of Indian Buddhism was ensured with the development, in the fifth century, of Tantra, a school of thought that emphasized ecstasy, ritual, and mystery, rather than solitary contemplation, and idealized sexual union as a means to triumph over the passions. Nevertheless, a few centuries later Buddhism had vanished from India almost as completely as had the Greeks, Huns, and Chinese.

Vedanta did not defeat Buddhism; no armies fought, no sages waved pamphlets. Buddhism simply subsided into

Vedanta, like water flowing back to the ocean from which it came. As Mahayana evolved, it became more and more similar to the religion from which it had parted; one could almost be a Buddhist and a Hindu simultaneously. And the flexible faith of Vedanta simply changed itself to resemble its rival: the Brahmans accepted a limited version of Tantra and elevated the primitive fertility goddesses—Lakshmi, Saraswati, and Parvati—into companions of the principal gods, thus adding a new element of romance, playfulness, and familiarity to the faith, as Mahayana had with the bodhisattvas. Buddha even became a Vedic god. Finally, as Vedanta proved flexible, so the caste system proved unshakable. It was all very well for a weaver to call himself a Buddhist, but unless he became a monk, and perhaps even if he did, he would continue to consider himself a member of the weaver caste, and so would others. The caste system was too important to a person's identity to be abandoned, and to be abandoned by it—to be declared an outcaste—was a terrifying prospect. Thus, like a Jain simply being restored to the caste system, a Buddhist never really left the fold. By the eighth century Buddhism had been largely absorbed into the old order.

IV The Moghul Empire

India was never long without a foreign invader; the period from roughly A.D. 1200 to 1750 saw the people of India prostrated before a succession of Central Asian Turks (the word refers not to the modern country of Turkey but to the nomadic tribes of the region), who finally succeeded in once more ruling the vast nation from a single capital. The second half of this period, known as the Moghul Empire, constitutes one of the great eras of Indian history. The Moghuls eventually collapsed like their predecessors. But Islam—a religion and a culture as powerful, if not as ancient, as Hinduism—had entered the country, and the two peoples adopted each other's customs, languages, and values. Neither absorbed the other, but both emerged changed.

To the ancient invaders India represented an opportunity to gain wealth and power; to the Muslim conquerors it offered, in addition, an insult to their religious faith. Followers of Islam, like the Christian Crusaders, bore a scripture in one hand and a sword in the other. Religious zeal made the Muslims relentless in attack, barbarous in victory, and persistent in their attempts to transform the nation. The first of the principal invaders, Mahmud Ghazni, known as the "idol-breaker," is said to have vowed to wage war against the Hindu infidels every year of his reign. Mahmud secured his glory in 1020 by slaughtering 50,000 unarmed pilgrims in the temple of Somnath and stealing its idol. The last of the Moghuls, Aurangzeb, destroyed the holiest of temples and raised mosques on the consecrated ground.

Throughout the thirteenth century a succession of Afghans known as the Slave Dynasty ruled northern India from Delhi. The throne was then taken forcibly by Alauddin, who became the first of the Muslim invaders to cross the mountains separating the north from the Deccan Plateau in the south, long unmolested by invasion. Alauddin was succeeded by Muhammad Tughlak, who, like many of the tribal rulers who followed him, combined merciless combat with a devout love of beauty. Tughlak surrounded himself with poets and artists and was himself a master of Persian verse and philosophy; but he had his enemies trampled to death and carved into ribbons by elephants with knives fixed to their tusks. Tughlak extended Alauddin's southern conquest and at one time controlled most of India, but local rebellions kept his empire in constant turmoil.

The succession of Feroze Shah, an Asoka-like king who

lived for his citizens, only accelerated the dissolution of this essentially Afghan conquest of India. In 1388, ten years after Feroze's death, Timur of Samarkand, whom the Western world knows as the invincible Tamburlaine, smashed the continental empire to bits in a few months, leaving Delhi a smoldering ruin, filled with the stench of rotting corpses.

The Moghul Empire, one of the most remarkable lines of kings the world has ever known, sprang directly from the loins of Timur. The marauder's fifth-generation descendant, Babur, inherited his crown in Turkestan. After defending his small possessions for twenty years, he made the startling decision to invade India with 12,000 men, although the armies he would face were huge. In his first battle, in 1526, he faced 100,000 troops led by the Sultan of Delhi. In half a day, with the famous Moghul cavalry charge, Babur left 15,000 of the enemy dead, and he gained the capital city. It took a bare three years for this military genius to bring all of northern India to submission. Babur's men were then ready to head for home with their plunder, and he found himself miserably homesick. Babur's court had been enriched by the art and culture of Persia; India, he complained, had "no good horses, no good meat, no grapes or melons," and its people lacked grace, intelligence, and talent. But Babur stood firm and died in this foreign land in 1530.

Babur's son Humayun almost frittered away the empire. Sunk in opium and drink, he allowed the Afghans to drive him all the way back to Kabul, where he had started. But the inevitable squabbling among the new rulers of Delhi produced such chaos that Humayun managed to conquer his way back in 1554.

Upon Humayun's death in 1556 the empire passed into the hands of the fourteen-year-old Akbar, then a spoiled boy in the harem. Over the next fifty years Akbar transformed the Moghul power from a court ruling from Agra to a great nation whose law and power were recognized throughout the continent. Akbar subdued his enemies, when called upon, with a ferocity worthy of the Turks: breaching the defenses of the great Chitor fort, in Gujarat, he slew 20,000 noncombatants and enslaved 20,000 more. But Akbar had the character of neither a despot nor a fanatic; like Asoka, he sought to bring harmony and justice in place of enmity and division.

Akbar's predecessors had been content to crush those they regarded as infidels and expand their authority over them. Akbar saw that tyranny of this sort made India not a nation but a collection of warring states barely held in check by a central power. The clash of Islam and Hinduism kept India in a state of hatred and fear. Yet the two peoples had mingled in the Moghul Empire—Akbar's own mother was a Hindu, and the Hindu Rajput warriors had long served Muslim rulers against Hindu princes—and Akbar believed that a rule of tolerance could begin to tear down the barriers that separated them. Akbar showed no favoritism to Muslims and counted Hindus among his closest advisers. His harem resembled the United Nations: Hindus, Persians, Moghuls, even an Armenian. He rescinded the hated *jizya,* a tax on Hindus. With an eye to justice he outlawed *suttee,* the practice of compelling Hindu widows to die on their husbands' funeral pyres; with an eye to religious harmony he permitted this practice if the woman had given full consent. Akbar burned no temples and broke no idols.

But mere administrative measures failed to bridle Akbar's far-reaching imagination or to satisfy his desire for greatness. To his new palace of Fatehpur Sikri, near Agra, he invited Muslims of all sects to engage in religious debate. Less and less satisfied with Islam, he expanded the group to include Christians, Jews, Zoroastrians, and Hindus, asking them to explain the essence of religious truth, to provide him with an equivalent of Asoka's Buddhism with which to rule the land. But Akbar's grand experiment turned into a sad comedy, with each divine abusing the others unmercifully. Akbar finally dismissed them all, fascinated by their doctrines but disgusted at their narrow-mindedness. Instead, in 1581, he announced the formation of the Divine Faith, a hopelessly artificial hodgepodge he had pieced together from the debates and his own speculation. As if this weren't horrifying enough to orthodox Muslims, he declared himself the prophet and pope of his universal religion. The Divine Faith never got past the court, where it was regarded as good form to swear to its truth; but Akbar's bold attempts at religious reform encouraged many Hindus to believe that they could live in peace with their conquerors.

Finally, Akbar, like Asoka, labored to bring a single system of laws and administration to the entire nation and to create harmony with justice. Akbar's brilliant adviser Todar Mal revamped the Moghul systems of governance and tax collection. Military leaders had been accustomed to paying for their upkeep by exacting, or extorting, what they needed from the peasantry. From Akbar's time, however, the government paid all military expenses, and its officers collected taxes. The vision of a spiritually united India may have eluded Akbar, as it has eluded those who succeeded him, but until the twentieth century no one did more than he to promote the idea of a nation among a skeptical people.

Great men rarely produce great sons. With Akbar's death the empire passed into the hands of Jahangir, who is said never to have gone to bed sober save on Friday nights, Friday being the Islamic Sabbath. Nevertheless, Jahangir fought well when he had to. But in court Jahangir let much of his power pass to his beautiful and ambitious wife, Nur Jahan. As Jahangir's health failed, his wife and her cronies plotted to enthrone a weakling who might prove easy to

Fatehpur Sikri, the ancient city near Agra where Akbar brooded over the world's religions (Photo courtesy of Government of India Tourist Board)

control. Jahangir's son Shahjahan, however, had other ideas, and a three-cornered civil war ensued, pitting the emperor against his own son. Shahjahan finally won, but not before much of the unity carefully nurtured by Akbar had slipped away.

Shahjahan spent much of the early part of his reign heading back and forth to the Deccan, whose leaders, Muslim as well as Hindu, proved generally unwilling to cooperate with the Moghuls; throughout India's history the South has asserted its independence from national governments. Nevertheless, the vast Moghul administrative system had reached the zenith of its efficiency, and Shahjahan was master of a staggering treasury. With these funds he not only furnished his court and army but built, in the mid-seventeenth century, the greatest monuments of the Moghul Empire. In Agra he built the Taj Mahal, the marble jewel of a crypt that housed the body of his wife and later that of Shahjahan himself. In Delhi he built the Red Fort, a gilded palace rather than a fort, and the Jama Masjid, the largest mosque in India. But despite a lifetime of glory Shahjahan ended like his father. Unable to choose a successor, he was finally imprisoned in his own palace by his son Aurangzeb, who took the throne by force.

The last of the great Moghuls, Aurangzeb, restored the ancient spirit of the *jihad*, the holy war against unbelievers. He resurrected the hated *jizya* and added to it a special sales tax for Hindus only; he burned down hundreds of temples, including the holiest shrines of Hinduism; and he carried out his attacks against Hindu strongholds like a man possessed. He transformed his own court from a gaudy, luxurious pleasure palace of free thinking to an austere encampment devoid of music and play. He himself knitted prayer caps and copied the Koran as signs of devotion. Aurangzeb proved the folly of Akbar's dream: the two faiths would live forever apart.

Aurangzeb's persecutions helped keep the pot of revolt boiling throughout northern India. The *jizya* and the emperor's fanaticism lessened the Rajputs' appetite for cooperation; though Aurangzeb succeeded in annexing the Rajput state of Rajasthan, he lost their assistance at a critical time. The Marathas, a hill tribe of the Deccan, had been harassing the Moghul armies, and thither Aurangzeb headed to subdue the sole threat to Moghul dominance in India. And there, twenty-five years later, he died, a broken man with a broken empire. The Marathas, like modern guerrillas, attacked from the hills, picked off the helpless Moghuls, and disappeared as suddenly as they had come. In his eighties Aurangzeb personally conquered and bribed his way into one fortress after another, but the Maratha horsemen only reappeared elsewhere. Aurangzeb's grand obsession drained strength from his army and, finally, himself. The north broke out in revolt; the Deccan could not be subdued. Aurangzeb died at eighty-nine, after writing to his son that "the soldiers are helpless, bewildered, and perturbed, like me. . . . Though I have a firm hope in God's grace, yet for my deeds anxiety ever remains with me."

With Aurangzeb's death the Moghul Empire went into a rapid decline, as the continental powers before it had done. The old Persian vices of luxury and drink paralyzed the court, while first the Marathas and finally the English extended their power. But the Moghul stamp was now firmly printed on the ancient nation. Two incompatible faiths now lived side by side, adjusting to one another, periodically fighting one another, as they do even now. Brahmans taught classical Persian to Muslims; the poetry, the painting, the language, and the philosophy of the closed, traditional Hindu world had been bombarded by the influence of another highly developed culture. The Muslims, at the same time, had learned to live with "infidels" and had even adopted castelike divisions. But beneath it all, the two religions remained intact, uneasy partners in a forced alliance.

V *The English Rule, Gandhian Resistance, the New Nation*

India had one more foreign conqueror to endure before the long centuries of bondage drew to a close. Europeans began to arrive in India in the sixteenth century (Marco Polo had stopped over on his way to China, admiring the horses and the textiles of the south), led by the seafaring nations of England and Portugal. England, then the world's foremost power, wrested control of the continent from the other

Europeans and quickly began to export the institutions—courts as well as clubs—that make up much of modern India. As the Moghuls "Persianized" India, so the English westernized it, though the English, with their arrogance and their permanent sense of homesickness, never mingled as previous conquerors had. The English brought India a unity it had never known before, governing every corner of the continent with their efficient civil service and their impartial court system. But, much to the surprise of the English, the Indians wanted the new nation for themselves, and they eventually kicked their masters out.

The British gained control of India gradually and almost accidentally. The British East India Company was established in 1600 to extract wealth from the new territory. The English thereby joined the Portuguese, the French, the Dutch, and even the Danes, all of whom had established trading posts on the Indian coastline. The company, though private, had troops from the Crown and used them, along with judicious bribery and a forged document, to capture Bengal. The company then began signing agreements with various princes who, as usual, were battling one another. The company's troops would intervene, carry the day often enough, and then sign a treaty guaranteeing control, or at least exclusive trading privileges, over the newly won territory. In this manner the company reduced its own allies to puppets and became the unofficial empire throughout India. By 1818 the British had defeated their only well-organized foes—Tipu, Sultan of Mysore, and the Marathas. Thus a small trading company with a few thousand troops at its disposal had gained the continent, a feat that recalled the exploits of Babur.

The British East India Company had been intended to set up factories and export silks and spices, not to take over a continent. But the English were happy to add India to their empire, and the East India Company was quickly replaced by governors and legislators. Delegations were sent to study local problems. England was experiencing a tidal wave of liberal reform in the early nineteenth century, and improving benighted India rapidly became "an outdoor sport for the middle classes," according to writer Francis G. Hutchins. Lord Macaulay, the great historian, recommended the adoption of a new educational system for the natives. Engineers honeycombed the continent with a railway network. Courts of law, rather than tyrannical will, resolved disputes. The Moghul revenue system was revamped. And from England's finest universities came the bureaucrats to run the new order with identical principles of efficiency and fairness guiding them from Kashmir to Madras. India had suffered a great deal in five millennia, but this bout of improvement was something entirely new.

The English naturally explained that their mission was philanthropical: they were shouldering "the white man's burden" of uplifting and Christianizing the dark masses. But the English were invaders no less than the Greeks, the Afghans, or the Moghuls had been. The English used their colonies as factories, as sources of raw materials and, finally, as new markets for goods made at home. Thus they "developed" India in a way that suited them. The educational system was designed not to wipe out illiteracy or provide technical skills but to create a privileged class to work with the English as civil servants, much the way the Moghuls used the Rajputs against their fellow Hindus. The railway system stretched from ports to factories or mines, and from cool hill stations to lowland English dwellings; it was not of much use to the average Indian. And the revenue system adopted in Bengal and Bihar gave a handful of landowners license to amass huge estates, so long as the English got their taxes.

Liberalism in India came to a screeching halt one day in January 1857 when troops supposedly loyal to the English opened fire on their masters in Bengal. In a matter of weeks the rebellion had spread as far as Punjab. Delhi fell into chaos. Englishmen along with their wives and children were butchered by their own servants and guards. The English, responding with equal ferocity, left rebels hanging from trees by the dozen and strapped others across cannons before firing. The English regained control by September, but they had been forced to act like conquerors rather than teachers, and never again would they feel perfectly secure. Thereafter the English granted reforms only when they felt they had no choice in the matter.

Nevertheless, the English continued to instill their basic values—the belief in democracy and in individual rights—in the few Indians they singled out for privilege. Members of this elite, known as "brown sahibs," sported fancy walking sticks, spoke Hindi only to their servants, quoted Shakespeare, and flattered the English whenever possible. But others began to feel that they had been paid off with the privilege of lording over their own people to remain servants of the British. What about democracy? In 1885 a group of Bengali intellectuals, the backbone of the colonial government, formed the Indian National Congress, with the goal of gaining increased self-rule. The Congress eventually became the revolutionary body that liberated India.

Democratic values were thoroughly alien to most Indians and served at first as a weak rallying point. But a "Hindu pride" movement rapidly gained enthusiasts. Scholars translated the epics, unearthing the ancient glories of Indian civilization, at a time when many people felt overwhelmed by the achievements of the West. Within Hinduism, a reform movement known as Arya Samaj tried to return the religion to its original Vedic purity. Swami Vivekenanda—a sage, scholar, and impassioned orator—aroused millions with his denunciation of mysticism and his interpretation of true Hinduism as truth, fearlessness, and clear-sightedness. Thus a system that had resisted change since civilization began suddenly became a force for nationalism and resistance rather than passivity and patience.

But the Congressmen envisioned a modern constitutional society, and the Samajists wanted a holy one. The two sides fought until they were fused together by the irresistible force of Mohandas K. Gandhi. Gandhi had studied in England and earned a law degree, but he was more prophet than lawyer. He shared with the Samajists a faith in the moral purity of the Indian people, a purity that the English had begun to corrupt. He wrote, "The beneficent institutions of the British government are like the fabled snake with a brilliant jewel on its head, but which has fangs full of poison." Gandhi believed that the English poison had to be extracted before the nation could be strong. He refused to wear English clothes, adopted a strict diet, and spun simple cotton on a wheel every morning. When he came to a village, the peasants saw a leader who had chosen to become one of them. Gandhi reached the people as no one before him had. Soon the dignified lawyers of the Congress burned their suits and spats and took up the spinning wheel.

Gandhi's message was a simple one: India had only to rediscover its own moral greatness—its spirit of selflessness and sacrifice, its powers of endurance, its dedication to truth and God, its ancient democratic institutions—to find the strength to defeat the British. Gandhi extracted the inner strength that had been buried beneath generations of passivity. First, Gandhi urged self-sufficiency: boycott foreign goods, English schools, English clubs. India could support itself. Then, in 1919, Gandhi initiated his campaign of *satyagraha,* nonviolent resistance. Indians would obstruct trains

Mohandas K. Gandhi, the prime mover of India's independence (Photo courtesy of the Indian Embassy to the United States)

or block factories, thereby forcing the British to arrest and perhaps brutalize them. Satyagraha demonstrated the moral strength of the victim and the cruelty of the state. The campaign continued until it turned violent in 1922, and then Gandhi called it off. "Suddenly," wrote Jawaharlal Nehru, later India's first prime minister, "that black pall of fear was lifted from people's shoulders, not wholly, of course, but to an amazing degree."

Gandhi spent relatively little time dickering with the British; he was more concerned with transforming his own people, using himself as an example to guide them toward moral strength. Gandhi was a shrewd dramatist; he knew how to catch his people's attention. In March 1930 he organized his famous Salt March. It had no specific political purpose; Gan-

Jawaharlal Nehru, the architect of free India—a student of Gandhi and his successor (Photo courtesy of the Indian Embassy to the United States)

dhi's goal was to embolden his people to defy the British by refusing to recognize their salt tax (as Americans once did with the tea tax). Gandhi walked 241 miles, from village to village, finally arriving at the Arabian Sea in Gujurat. There he picked up a handful of salt from the seaside. It was only a symbol of defiance, but the image of a frail, aging man walking through the blazing sun to scoop up a handful of salt thrilled millions of Indians and, thanks to international news coverage, excited the imagination of the world.

The English hardly knew how to deal with such a gentle but implacable revolt. At times they tried to satisfy Congress by increasing Indian representation in the provincial and national legislatures. By 1935 the Congress had gained control of most of the provincial assemblies, so that in the eyes of villagers Congress had already become the legitimate government. But the British also felt that they could not cave in before the Congress, and they periodically cracked down with widespread arrests and beatings. A major campaign of satyagraha, declared in 1932, collapsed when Gandhi and every other major leader was immediately arrested.

Gandhi dropped out of the movement after his release from prison in 1934, as he had after 1922, leaving the direction of the Congress to younger and less patient men like Nehru. Gandhi realized that the hunger for independence had overtaken his moral experiments. Agitation continued throughout the 1930s, with Gandhi on the sideline. When the British entered World War II in 1939, the viceroy, Lord Linlithgow, announced that India had joined the war. The Indians, however, thought otherwise. Nehru offered to cooperate in exchange for an offer of independence after the war. The English refused—Churchill had pledged never to surrender the empire—and instead decided to crush the Congress. The Emergency Powers Ordinance of 1940 banned all "anti-British" activities. British soldiers raided villages believed to contain Congress sympathizers. In 1942 the government carried out mass arrests. Gandhi then announced the Quit India campaign. A massive program of civil disobedience got under way, crippling the railroads, cutting telephone wires, destroying government property. Rioters in Bihar battled soldiers with spears, bows and arrows, and elephants. Gandhi was unable to prevent repeated outbreaks of violence because he was in jail. For this reason the Quit India campaign is often regarded as Gandhi's greatest failure. Nevertheless, it succeeded in the long run. The British realized that their support in India had evaporated, and they met with Indian leaders to plan a total transfer of power. Gandhi was not involved; he had symbolized to India what it wanted to become and had given it the courage to reach for that ideal.

To millions of non-Indians the memory of Gandhi remains as proof that peace and charity can be powerful instruments of social change. Many American political leaders of the 1960s acknowledged a great debt to Gandhi; foremost among them was Martin Luther King, whose civil disobedience campaign for civil rights was explicitly modeled on Gandhi's movement.

Handing over India posed two major problems. First, who were the British going to hand it over to? The British had always let the princes rule their own states. Were they to be included in the new India? More pressing, however, was the Muslim problem. Thirty percent of India's millions were Muslim, and many of them feared that if Hindus ruled India, the Muslims would be ill-treated. The Muslim League had formed in 1906 as a counterweight to the overwhelmingly Hindu Congress. The league tried to protect Muslim power by guaranteeing a minimum number of Muslim seats in the assemblies. At first the league resisted independence, then its long-time leader, M. A. Jinnah, came up with the idea of dividing an independent India into two parts—a Hindu nation, India, and an Islamic one, Pakistan. Jinnah began his "Islam in danger" campaign in the late 1930s, convincing Muslims that their safety could be secured only through the creation of a separate state. With this goal in mind Jinnah sabotaged one independence plan after another; and when the British sided with Jinnah, trying to force the Congress into a compromise, Congress held back.

The Congress bitterly opposed any partition. The English considered partition unnecessary, but mostly wanted to leave the whole mess as soon as possible. In August 1946 the viceroy asked Nehru to assume leadership of the government of India. Jinnah retaliated by declaring "direct action day" to agitate for a Muslim nation. In a terrible omen India's first major religious riots broke out; five thousand people were killed in Calcutta in two days. Pressure rose to create a separate state, and when the new English negotiator, Lord Mountbatten, arrived in March 1947, partition already seemed inevitable. Mountbatten quickly secured agreement to lop off the northern half of Punjab and the eastern half of Bengal. Pakistan thus was born.

But few nations have been born with so much bloodshed. Hindus fleeing Pakistan and Muslims fleeing India were slaughtered by their religious enemies. Sikhs in Punjab climbed aboard trains headed for Pakistan and murdered everyone on board. Half a million people died in the uncontrollable riots, far more than the British killed in two centuries. Upon its birth India presented to the world a confusing spectacle: a nation unified against an enemy by the profound spirit of satyagraha, but divided against itself by rivers of blood.

3
Daily Life

I The Village Scene

The life of the average Indian villager, depending on your point of view, either has barely changed since the invention of the plow or has undergone a revolution in the years since independence. Casual visitors to the countryside would probably draw the first conclusion. In the fields they would see a bony man wrapped in a loincloth guiding an ox back and forth over stony ground, preparing the soil for his acre or two of wheat; along the dusty back roads they might see a long file of women in faded saris with vast piles of branches perched on their heads, making the long trip to market. The village would appear as a rough assemblage of mud huts slapped up out of the same ancient dust from which a hundred generations of identical huts had risen. More experienced observers, however, might see something else. They might notice that the farmer's ox cart had metal ball bearings, an expensive change allowing the ox to drag a heavier

load, that the dusty path the women used led after only two
miles to a paved road served by a bus, that the peace of the
village was shattered by the sound of a radio, and that a brick
primary school rose at the edge of the village. Both groups of
onlookers would be right, for the story of the Indian village
is one of extraordinary continuity only recently disturbed by
striking change.

The typical village, like the typical anything, exists only in
the imagination. Villages vary depending on climate, crops,
region, and income. Punjabis dare visitors to find a mud hut
among the spread-out communities of brick and mortar
homes. In the south peasants build their homes of wattle—
dried-out palm fronds tightly woven and supported by
wooden poles. Homes are often surrounded by private gardens of banana trees, papaya trees, and palms. The village
that we will describe here might be glimpsed in the "Hindi
heartland"—the populous, Hindi-speaking area stretching
from Bihar in the east to Rajasthan or even Gujarat in the
west.

Few villages are visible from the occasional paved road
that crosses the countryside; seen from the window of a
passing bus India looks practically empty. But a path, navi-
gable by jeep or at least by bicycle, stretches from the road
into an invisible interior. The first village may be only a few
hundred yards away; beyond it the path winds on and on,
through village after village, apparently without end. Peasants live not next to their land but cheek by jowl with one
another, trooping out to the fields at dawn.

The home of a poor peasant consists of little besides four
mud walls. Since the door may be nothing more than a
rectangle cut in the mud, and windows would be an open
invitation to wind and rain, the hut will remain almost completely dark throughout the day. Electricity is inconceivable.
The only belongings are the few indispensable ones. A pile

of gunny sacks with rice or flour may lie in a corner. For bedding the family may have a few sacks, or a straw mattress, and possibly a *charpoy,* or string cot. The charpoy often sits just outside the hut, ready for visitors who come by for a smoke at the end of the day. Everyone in the family may have a change of clothes or two. A few precious objects, perhaps wedding gifts like bangles or even jewelry, may be locked up in a box or trunk. There is probably little else.

Owing to the lack of space, as well as the heat, villagers spend far more time outside than in. Food is generally cooked and eaten in a courtyard behind the hut, often a common area shared by a number of families. The cow or buffalo, if the family is lucky enough to own one, may have its own claims on the courtyard, since animals are usually quartered in sheds behind the hut. And, except in cold weather, the family will drag the charpoy and the bedding back to the courtyard, and sleep beneath the stars.

Although starvation is quite rare in India, poor villagers live with hunger almost every day of their lives. The staple food of north India is bread, but many poor farmers make bread not from the wheat they grow but from sorghum, a cheaper and far rougher crop. The peasant's wife pounds the ground flour into flat cakes called *chappatis,* which will be eaten with rice or a soup of lentils, known in India as *dal.* The sorghum or wheat and dal will come from the farmer's own crop, and poor peasants often grow little more than their family eats. Those who also grow vegetables try to save them for the market, but the family may also eat some of the onions, carrots, cauliflower, or whatever the farmer grows. Similarly, the purpose of a cow or buffalo is to give milk to sell in town, but peasants with small children try to keep some of the milk for them. To eat meat is out of the question not so much for religious reasons as for economic ones; no farmer would think of slaughtering his only buffalo for meat, nor could he afford to buy the meat at the butcher's. It is, overall, a diet short on calories, short on protein and, usually, short on bulk, since many peasants eat only twice a day.

Every village has a very clear economic hierarchy. At the bottom are the farm laborers, who own no land of their own but till someone else's acreage for perhaps a dollar a day or less. Then come the sharecroppers, who work another man's land, not for a daily wage but for a fixed percentage of the crop that they grow. Many of them own a little bit of land, say an acre or so—not enough to support their whole family. At the top are the self-supporting landowners, who may have anywhere from two acres to two hundred. A peasant with a half-dozen acres or more is a member of the village middle class. He will probably own a brick home, think about sending his child to high school, and travel into town every once in a while. And practically every village has one or two large landowners, with twenty-five acres or more. These grandees often live in two-story homes that have carved doorways and painted pillars and are built around a courtyard, with rooms opening all around. They may own a motorcycle or even a car, and sport silk pajama suits or saris. Rich peasants often double as moneylenders and judges; no one dares question their ultimate control of the village.

In very large villages a fair number of men may not work in the fields at all. Some may teach, others may work at crafts or small-scale industries. But most small villages have very few tasks for the nonfarmer. Every village has a *dhobi*, or washerman, who washes clothes in water drawn from a well or irrigation canal and pounds them dry on rocks. Nowadays it is also common for villages to have a primary school teacher and an accountant, or treasurer, both sent by the government, who often live in the nearest town. And though most shopping must be done in a market that serves thousands of people, a moderately up-to-date village is likely to have a shopkeeper who sells packaged foods, possibly a few plastic items, pots, cups, plates, rope, and even birth-control devices. To his stock of native cigarettes, or *bidis*, he may add packs of Gold Coin or Golconda, which Indians smoke by cupping the hand before the mouth and jamming the cigarette between the third and fourth finger.

Small villages don't generally provide enough work for shoemakers, barbers, blacksmiths, and the like, so the villagers must wait until one of these figures arrives every few months or even years. Farmers save up their bent and shattered tools until the blacksmith suddenly comes rolling into the village's dusty main square. This is an event so dramatic that the work of the village may temporarily come to a halt. The blacksmith and his family may travel all across northern India, and arrive with tales of strange places that leave the farmers agape. The women of his family, accustomed to wielding hammers and fending for themselves, laugh boldly and speak to the village men in tones the men have never heard before. The village children gather around and stare at the elaborately decorated ox cart in which the family travels. In many Indian villages a visit like this may be the closest thing to the arrival of the circus.

The actual work of farming is both exhausting and irregular. Only the wealthiest farmers can think of spending 500 dollars or more for a tractor, which, in any case, can't be used efficiently on less than 20 or so acres. Some of the more well-to-do farmers may rent a tractor at planting time. But for the rest the plowing must be done by a pair of yoked oxen, just as it was done a thousand years ago and more; the harvesting must be done by hand. Often plots are broken up into tiny pieces, practically gardens, of a quarter-acre or even less, thus making the work of sowing and reaping even more difficult. And in that quarter-acre a farmer may grow half a dozen crops—potatoes, onions, carrots, eggplants, dal, mustard, and so on.

Relatively few farmers can grow crops year-round, because they have no supply of water. Throughout northern India it rains only between mid-June and mid-September. At that time of the year, known as the monsoon season, the rainfall is virtually unceasing, often causing floods in which a whole village can be washed away like a house of cards. The summer crop is normally harvested after the rainy season. Many farmers can grow a small vegetable crop in the winter, but as the months wear on the lack of rain parches the earth. If the village tank is depleted early the crop may not survive. Only farmers lucky enough to live near a large and dependable irrigation system can think about growing a third crop in the spring, when not a cloud crosses the sky for months on end and the temperature may reach 115 degrees.

II Family and Social Life

Back at home the women have it no easier. Awake at four or five o'clock, they must grind two or three pounds of flour for the day's chappatis, collect dried dung for the fire, draw water from the well, make bread for their husbands' lunch, and take it to them in the field. Much the same routine must be repeated in the afternoon. The life of Indian women, especially in the north, is hidden behind a veil—quite literally. Once they are married Indian women are not supposed to be seen by men except their relatives and husband. When they see a man walking toward them down one of the village's narrow alleys married women, who always seem to walk in groups, will flip their veil over their head. To draw them into conversation is almost impossible; the veil cuts them off from the world as much as it protects them from it.

The wives of the agricultural laborers may work beside these poorest of peasants in the fields, as may the children. For any other woman work in the fields would be too demeaning to consider, save perhaps at harvest time. But there is no other work for her to do. Once she is married, and often beforehand, a girl's education generally comes to a stop. She will almost never leave home until she is married. Girls know that there is nothing for them to become save wives and mothers, so even the tiniest ambitions seem silly.

The life of a little boy, on the other hand, is almost enviable. Indian parents always pray for a boy: he will bring a dowry in marriage, he will shoulder the burden of his aging father. Indian population control laws exempt parents to whom only girls have been born: they can try again a third or fourth time. Boys grow up surrounded by women—mother, sisters, aunts, grandmothers, neighbors—all of whom coddle him and grant his every wish. No relationship in an Indian family is as close as that of a boy, or a man, to his mother. But the boy does not remain the center of attention for long, at least not in the villages. A proverb says, "Treat your son as a raja until he is five, a slave until he is fifteen, and then as a friend." As soon as he can wield a stick and lift a stone the boy is sent to watch over the cattle, buffalo, or goats or to help his father in the field. The women still try to spoil him, but his father sees to it that he takes his work seriously.

Not only in the villages but also in the towns and cities Indians live in what is called the "joint family system." A young man, unless he moves to a new area, will remain with his wife in his parents' home. As his parents grow old he will support them, keeping them in his home and deferring to them in many important decisions. Gradually the household may expand to include childless uncles, widowed sisters, even a lazy cousin; relatives simply cannot be turned away.

A peasant preparing to till his fields (Photo courtesy of the Indian Embassy to the United States)

The poor in villages build another room on their huts; the immensely wealthy in cities add another wing to their home or another home in their compound; but the home in any case must expand to serve the family. The services that the United States and European nations have developed to free the young of the burden of elderly parents and children—social security, nursing homes, day-care centers—seem to Indians to show a lack of personal responsibility. Even with

their pressing financial problems they would rather sink with their family, by and large, than surrender anyone to the care of the government.

Marriage is the most important event in the life of the family. Though it seems odd to us, an Indian marriage weighs much less heavily on the bride and groom than on their parents. Young people do not choose spouses for themselves, in fact, even today, couples rarely meet before the wedding ceremony. When a child reaches fourteen or fifteen the father, or sometimes the mother, starts hunting for a suitable mate. The search is bound to be an arduous one, because not only two individuals but two families will be bound together. The parent may range over two dozen villages trying to find the right family. Marriage within the village or between members of neighboring villages is rarely permitted. First and foremost, the families must belong to the same caste. To marry below your caste is a disgrace; to marry above it is almost impossible without some rare distinction, such as a large inheritance or a college education. A proper marriage affirms the family's place in the caste system; an improper one violates dharma and confuses a person's place in the world.

The father will have a great many questions to ask. He will want to know how well off the family is and will ask about its local reputation, its habits, its relations. If he is pursuing a bride for his son, he will scrutinize the young woman to see that she is well behaved and modest. Perhaps his wife will accompany him to conduct an inquiry into the girl's domestic talents. If he seeks a husband for his daughter, the father will ask about the young man's education and work prospects. A son fetches a dowry—a gift from the girl's parents to his own—proportional to his value as a husband. The dowry may be a buffalo, a motorbike, or a radio. An Indian marriage may sound to us like a rather cold-blooded economic transaction, but we should keep in mind that the functions of such a marriage are to cement the bonds of caste and to unite two families, two villages, two communities.

Marriage ceremonies have the unfortunate side effect of practically bankrupting both sides. The dowry and the trousseau empty the purse of the daughter's family, while the celebration itself does the same to the bridegroom's family. Hundreds of relatives and guests may have to be fed, shel-

A wedding, with the dowry—a radio—placed before the couple
(Photo courtesy of Air India)

tered, and entertained. A band must be hired, as well as a horse, or even an elephant, for the marriage procession from the groom's house to the bride's. A Brahman priest must be fed and paid, for it is he who will conduct the ritual itself, chanting ancient hymns before a sacred fire, around which the new couple will walk seven times to affirm their faith. Poor families must go into debt to the local shopkeeper or landlord in order to pay for the elaborate festivities; and, with interest running at 30 percent a year and up, the debt may never be repaid.

III The Caste System

Caste rules the life of the villager, not only in marriage but in work and in leisure. In India a man does not choose his occupation; he is born into it. When he sits over a pipe in the evening, he passes it to a fellow caste member, someone of the same standing; when festival time comes around he celebrates with others of the same rank; and when he goes to the polls, it is assumed, sometimes wrongly, that he will vote for someone of his own caste.

The caste system has been developing for three or four thousand years, more than enough to become complicated almost beyond human understanding. At first society was divided into four castes: priests, warriors, tradesmen, and workers, a category later divided into "clean" and "unclean." In order to keep pace with changes in society the caste system continually absorbed new occupations, new distinctions. The four basic divisions began to lose meaning as they were overtaken by thousands of different caste groups.

Nowadays no Indian would identify himself as, for example, a kshatriya, or warrior. India no longer even has a warrior caste, since the army is open to all castes. The descendants of the old warriors are now India's wealthiest landowners. And there are hundreds of such landowning castes: Rajputs, Thakurs, Jagirdars (a name that actually means "landholder"). The name of the caste varies from place to place, but members consider one another social equals, more or less. All of these "forward caste" or "high caste" members look down on the "backward castes"—the thousands of groups of small landowners, craftsmen, laborers. And they, in turn, look down upon the Untouchables, so called because their very touch was once considered polluting. Even today most upper-caste peasants would not eat food cooked by an Untouchable.

The Indian Constitution has officially abolished caste distinctions, but it might as well have tried to abolish the summer. In most villages caste continues to mean everything, and many of its most cruel elements have scarcely changed at all. Landless laborers, most of them Untouchables, are often attached, by tradition, to an upper-caste family and farm. A laborer will often fall deeply in debt to a farmer and is then obliged to keep working for the farmer until he pays off his debt, which he may never do. This practice, akin to slavery, is called bonded labor, and flourishes despite having been prohibited by the Constitution. A bonded laborer cannot work elsewhere unless he runs away from the village. And unless he finally pays off the debt his son will inherit his obligation. Thus the power of the ruling castes over the lower castes is reinforced from generation to generation.

The obligation runs both ways, however. The high-caste farmer must supply a loan when the peasant needs it to tide him over during periods of illness or inactivity. Only because the obligation is shared does the system survive, and only because the poor peasant or potter or barber believes in it as much as the well-to-do employer does the obligation continue to run both ways. They do not sign a contract, as they would in the United States; the Indian village runs on shared values, with the mighty as well as the humble believing in the system that binds them together. This unofficial agreement certainly works out better for the mighty than for the humble, since it keeps everyone in his place. Nevertheless, the sense of security and protection it gives to those on the bottom is no small consideration for a people constantly menaced by disease, floods, drought and, until recently, strangers.

IV New Sights, New Thoughts, New Hopes

But this traditional picture of the Indian village is too neat. Generations of invaders left the countryside pretty much the way they found it, but thirty years of self-rule have brought more change, intended and unintended, good and bad, than many past centuries combined. The powerful bonds of the caste system have lost some of their force as villagers have been able to pedal bicycles down new paths and roads into town, there to find work, sell fruits or vegetables or wood, talk with villagers from far away, walk down broad streets lined with shops, watch the brilliant lights go on at night. Though it is still rare to find a prosperous Untouchable in a village, many of the worst marks of untouchability have begun to fade. Harijans, as they are also called— the word means "God's children," and was coined by Gandhi—may now draw water from the same well, or worship in the same temple, as other castes. Certainly their children may sit in the same classroom with Brahmans and Thakurs. Still, every village has its Harijan quarter, its cluster of shabby mud huts; not for a very long time will it be otherwise.

Increased contact with nearby towns has brought money into village life. Until recently the lower castes worked for the higher castes as an obligation; the higher castes supported them as their obligation. There were no contracts, and no money was exchanged. Now the two sides have begun to bargain with one another, like factory owners and their workers. Laborers are paid so much per day instead of receiving whatever they need in grain and clothing. Should they fall sick, they can no longer automatically expect the landlord to pay their bills. Workers, however, enjoy a bit more bargaining power, since they can threaten to find work elsewhere (usually a fairly distant possibility). The same high castes continue to own the land and the shops, and the same low castes continue to labor for them, but the ancient glue that has bound them together—the belief that their religion obliges them to do what they do for one another—has begun to weaken. And this, as we will see later, has led not only to freedom but to great suffering.

Communication, no less than transportation, has begun to change the spirit of the village. Indians with radios are connected to an enormous world. As children they grew up with local folk songs and religious hymns; now they hear popular tunes recorded in a big city hundreds of miles away, songs with words that reflect sophisticated urban values, music that has a raucous, exciting, electric beat. News broadcasts bring them information about people and countries they have never heard of, about wars and revolutions and great events. They hear about the political parties jousting in Delhi or the state capital, hear their promises and grow excited or perhaps cynical. They hear about villages throughout the vast continent, connected somehow to them and their village, and they come to think of themselves as not only Jats or Bhumihars or Punjabis or Keralites but as Indians. Radios have probably promoted nationalism more successfully than great leaders have.

And movies! Villagers have only to walk to the nearest town of any size to sit beneath a tent on a rickety chair and witness amazing Technicolor tales of beautiful heroines, indomitable young men, cruel, insensitive fathers, and evil schemers. The films are just like the old legends, except that in the movies people throw unimaginable sums of money around on cars and liquor and gambling, characters wear Western clothes and live in big houses with modern furniture, and sometimes the nattily dressed lawyers and businessmen on the screen will say a few words in English: "Bye now," or "a cool million," or "basic problem." It's no wonder that movies in India are wildly popular; they send the imagination of the average viewer reeling. Bombay might as well be a legendary city of the past to most villagers, but once they have seen it in a movie, the villagers feel that the city and its immense possibilities are close at hand.

But for hundreds of thousands of rural Indians the most exciting technology is undoubtedly television. Although only a tiny handful of peasants have the income to buy a television set for themselves, in the early 1980s the Indian government embarked on a program to bring the medium into as many villages as possible. Several thousand villages across the country now have sets, and most of them receive programming—news, film clips, educational shows, tips on farming and health—by means of a radar dish pointed at a satellite. India has few stranger sights to offer than that of a crowd of peasants in a village with not a dozen light bulbs, sitting cross-legged beneath the stars, illuminated by the glow of a television set.

The effect of all these changes on the average villager's way of thinking is staggering, though impossible to calculate. Many ideas that have been blindly accepted since time out of mind are being called into question, if not rejected outright. Through the media the government has been able to preach against social ills like untouchability, dowry, bonded labor, the pitiable condition of women, even the unresponsiveness and corruption of the government itself. Villagers have come to know more and more about politics, and make more independent choices. The crushing burden of resignation—the belief that nothing can be changed—is being lifted, inch by inch.

The physical as well as the mental life of the village has undergone great change in the recent past. Charlotte Wiser, an American social scientist, lived in the village of Mainpuri, in Uttar Pradesh, in 1930; she returned in 1960 and again in 1970. On her 1960 visit she noticed that every house in the village belonged to the same family that had owned it thirty years before, but the village now had a cycle-repair shop and a sweet shop at the bus stand—both signs that the villagers had become more mobile. And, in fact, the peasants had begun trading in the town for the first time. When she returned in 1970, Wiser found that educational opportunities had given new hope to people long resigned to remaining in place. High school education had become common, and fifteen villagers were enrolled in college. Most amazing of all was the news that a Brahman and a shepherd boy had left the village for Delhi, where they were sharing a home. A new prosperity had come to the village: forty homes were now *pukka*, or solid, made from brick and mortar; dowry gifts had risen from bicycles to watches to transistor radios, and new seeds, fertilizer, and irrigation systems had made the land yield far more crops. On her last visit Wiser summarized these changes in the progress made in providing light. Long ago the only source of light was torches made of oil-soaked rags fixed to sticks; these gave way to clay saucers with cotton wicks floating in oil; these to oil lamps and then to lanterns; then to the Petromax, a popular and powerful lamp that burns gas made from kerosene; and finally to the electric lights that had begun appearing by her last visit. Observers have to look closely to see the changes in village life, but if they do, they will realize the silliness of the tourist's notion that India is a land where everything always remains the same.

V Town and City

Only 20 percent of the Indian people live in towns and cities of 5,000 people or more, but that small fraction represents 140 million people—more than the population of all but five countries in the world. The bulk of these urban Indians live not in great cities but in towns with anywhere from 20,000 to 200,000 citizens.

Small and medium-sized towns have much in common with the villages that surround them: cows wander through the streets, washermen bang clothing against rocks in nearby streams, homes built of mud and tar paper and corrugated tin and planks and cardboard lean against one another, ready to be toppled by the first big storm. But the pace of the Indian town nearly terrifies the villager. The streets are often a wild free-for-all, with buses bearing down on pedestrians, dogs and goats scurrying out of the way of three-wheeled taxis and cars, bicycles weaving past the carters who wearily push their loads of flour sacks uphill—and the air filled with the sounds of beeping horns, shouts and snatches of conversation, and the rattle and bang of old contraptions.

But the visitor soon learns that no one is in a hurry. If a car breaks down, the driver and passengers, instead of drumming their fingers angrily on the hood, head for the nearest tea shop patiently to await the arrival of the repairman. Cloth salesmen sit cross-legged in their open shops gazing out at passersby; when a serious customer arrives the salesman calls for a cup of tea or a soft drink (a modern option) and begins throwing one bolt of cloth after another across his lap. If the customer declines to buy anything, the shopkeeper merely shrugs and begins the long process of folding the silk and cotton that surround him. After dusk the air grows thick with the smoke of fires built along the roadside, while a soft jangle of bells marks the departure of the ox carts.

The Indian city conjures up, in the minds of foreigners, an image of horror: beggars and cripples, clouds of insects, millions of men and women jostling one another through the streets. This impression is not totally wrong; it's simply incomplete. Cities throughout the so-called developing world—the poor nations—face a crushing problem: nobody wants to stay on the farm. With low wages and scarce job opportunities, the countryside can scarcely compete with the lure of the big city, especially the fantasy version presented in the movies. Every day, cities in India, as well as elsewhere in Asia, Latin America, and Africa, absorb thousands of hopeful villagers for whom they have no place.

In a city like Bombay, with its back against the Arabian Sea and little room to expand, most of the eight million residents live crowded together in rickety two- or three-story dwellings, cramped into tiny rooms hardly bigger than a bed, without running water, with a few tattered articles of clothing hanging from nails in the wall. The well-to-do are stacked into astronomically expensive apartment complexes, where rent often absorbs half a person's salary or more.

All Indian cities are crowded. A vast ocean of people seems to wash back and forth across the streets from early morning until late at night. The roads are lined with vendors squatting behind displays of sweets, cheap paperbacks, gaudy calendars, fruits and vegetables. Standing on the street corner you can have your hair cut, your shoes shined, your ears cleaned. Astonishing numbers of people are crammed into buses, with a small knot invariably hanging from handrails on the outside. Certain items—stamps, train tickets, beer—can be purchased only after waiting in seemingly endless lines. Urban life gives Indians a great opportunity to demonstrate their famous patience.

The impression that Indian cities are overgrown towns is not quite accurate. Two major cities have been built in the twentieth century—New Delhi in the north and Bangalore in the south—and both are clean and orderly, bisected by broad avenues through which traffic flows neatly, if incessantly. The sizable middle class lives in carefully laid out "colonies," or neighborhoods ringing the downtown area, and parks and gardens provide a constant relief. Modern government buildings dominate the heart of town, while relatively sophisticated factories stand along the outskirts. Expensive hotels and restaurants cater to foreigners and wealthy Indians not only in these two cities but also in Calcutta, Madras, and Bombay.

But few city dwellers will ever see the inside of these

buildings; most work in difficult conditions and draw tiny salaries. The better-off work as clerks in government offices or business, or labor in factories; they may earn as much as 100 dollars a month. The less fortunate try to hawk their wares on street corners or wash dishes in the heat among the flies of a tea shop or look around for temporary work or beg. There simply isn't enough work to go around. Families who can't afford even the little shacks that shoulder one another in shantytowns often stake out a space beneath a bridge or overpass. Others simply live on the street, sleeping in the shadow of the tall buildings. The streets of Calcutta, the only city in India where men, rather than horses, bicycles, or engines, still pull passengers around town, are not only impassable by day but crowded by night with the people who live there. Beggary is rampant and desperate.

Poverty in the city must be far harder to endure than poverty in the country. The peasant and the pencil seller may be getting by on the same scanty meals, but the peasant has never had to watch people walk out of restaurants patting their stomachs. The same longing for freedom that drove the villagers to the city now makes them feel abandoned. They have lost the protection of their age-old world, lost the sense of familiarity and harmony. Now they live in a strange and hostile place where few people know them and passersby bump into them on the street. But how can they go back to their villages? They have seen firsthand the world that their old friends know only through movies; they have seen streets blazing with light; and even the bitterness they feel watching the well-fed emerging from their restaurants binds them to the city with a dream of its possibilities.

The big city holds two classes of people not found elsewhere in India: the homeless, despairing poor and the Westernized upper class. Indians with good jobs in government, business, and the professions share many of the manners and

attitudes of Englishmen and Americans, for the English left
their stamp on India as surely as did the Moghuls. Indians
born into good families generally go to English-language
schools, watch English movies, and play English sports like
cricket and soccer. With one another they are more likely to
speak English than their regional language. They wear
Western-style suits, drink cocktails, and attend Sunday-
afternoon lawn parties. They study the literature and politics
of Europe and America, often more closely than Europeans
or Americans do. Those with enough money travel abroad or
send their children to college in England or the United
States. India has no more withering critics than its own urban upper-class lawyers and businessmen, who frequently
abuse their fellow citizens for inefficiency, soft-headedness,
and indolence.

Westernized Indians share few of the nation's traditional
values. Orthodox Hinduism forbids the crossing of "the
black waters"—the ocean. But they, in fact, look abroad for
values and ideas. Middle-class Indians pay far less attention
to caste than do villagers and townspeople, though in their
social life they may spend most of their time with members
of their own caste. Young people sometimes choose their
own husbands or wives, though even very Westernized Indians are surprisingly willing to permit their parents to ar-
range matches for them. The difficulty of finding spacious
housing and the desire for freedom have reduced the popularity of the joint family, though young couples more often
than not move in with the husband's parents. Above all,
these "new" Indians consider themselves unfettered by the
ancient commandments of religion; Nehru himself confessed
to having no faith in the existence of God. Others who would
not go so far would say that they are guided in their daily acts
by the rule of reason, not by the dictates of religion or tradition. Of course, they would probably be exaggerating a bit.

India really consists of two cultures—another of its myriad divisions. One culture lives in big cities, speaks English, and looks to the "modern" West for inspiration and values; the other lives in the towns and villages, speaks one of the native tongues, and looks to its own past for guidance. Only a tiny fraction of the Indian people belongs to the first group, but they not only run the government and much of the business enterprise, they also make the movies, publish the glossy magazines, and write the advertising that provide people with images of the good life. Yet the visions of happiness that they produce—and believe—reflect the lifestyle of only a handful of Indians. The sophisticated city dwellers probably have more in common with the traditional villager than they think, but the two hold such different values that they have trouble communicating with one another. And this failure, as we shall see later, has helped complicate some of India's gravest problems.

4

Hinduism and Its Rival Religions

People who write about India have a hard time avoiding phrases like "Hindu society" and "the Hindu order." The problem with these terms is that they usually refer not only to Hindus but to all Indians. No other word is suitable to describe the basic values and social system that have been preserved over generations. Only recently, in fact, has the word "Hindu" come to mean the religion of 80 percent of Indians; years ago it was used vaguely to refer to the life, culture, and values of the people who lived in India; what we now call Hinduism was known by other names, such as Vedanta. Where we speak of "American" values, scholars refer to "Hindu" values; the word "India" was invented two centuries ago by the British, and Indians now refer to their country as "Hindustan." We must recall, in spite of all this linguistic confusion, that 200 million Indians profess Islam, Sikhism, Buddhism, Christianity, or Zoroastrianism, and that India has justly been called "the mother of religions."

I *Hinduism*

Hinduism, like the religions of ancient Greece and Rome, developed an entire family of gods. After a number of centuries three gods became dominant and have since been worshiped all over India under thousands of different names; they are Siva, Vishnu, and Brahma. Siva (pronounced SHEE-va) is the god of destruction, dispatching demons with a splendid bow shot or whirling into an awesome and hypnotizing dance to bring the end of the world. A god of creation and sexual power as well, Siva is worshiped in the form of a lingam, or phallus. Vishnu is the preserver, the protector of man and all life. In one of his many incarnations he appears on earth as Krishna, a playful boy-god who plays the flute, teases girls, and tips over pitchers of milk onto the heads of milkmaids when the mood strikes him. Brahma is not seen in such familiar terms; he is associated with the beginning of the universe, which Hinduism, anticipating modern science, traditionally placed at several billion years in the past.

Both Siva and Vishnu have their adherents (though all Hindus believe in the three gods), and stories grew up to explain the precedence of one or the other. Vishnu and Brahma are said to have been sitting around one day before the creation of the world, arguing over who was the more important. All of a sudden a brilliant pillar of light shot up before their eyes, leaving them speechless. Brahma, in the form of a boar, investigated the source, while Vishnu, as an eagle, flew up to the summit. But they found that the gleaming pillar had neither bottom nor top. As they stood there contemplating their own insignificance, the pillar opened up and out stepped Siva, thus settling the argument of who was greatest among the gods.

The Hindu gods enjoy love and humor and experience envy, just as humans do. Siva and his lovely consort Parvati while away much of their time gambling; a sculpture in the famous caves of Ellora shows Siva encircling his beloved's waist with one arm and pushing her hands away from the dice with another (he has four), preventing her from going double or nothing. Vishnu, appearing in the form of a dwarf, challenges a demon. The demon laughingly grants the dwarf's request that he be permitted to take three steps. Shooting up beyond all measure, Vishnu crushes the demon with his first stride, crosses the world with his second, and straddles the universe with his third, thus convincingly indicating who's boss.

Stories like these illuminate the world for the Indian people. From an early age they hear long tales spun out from the ancient epics, the *Mahabharata* and the *Ramayana*, as well as all sorts of legends about local gods (of whom there are hundreds of thousands). They see the same tales acted out at festivals and come to know them by heart. Gandhi understood the importance of these stories and often recalled moments of courage from the epics in order to give heart to a crowd of villagers. And the villagers, in turn, placed Gandhi alongside their own legendary heroes, calling him Mahatma, or "Great Soul." Hindus cannot understand the sharp distinction most of us draw between the world of religion—of gods, miracles, and ultimate moral truths—and daily life; for them, as for most people who are dependent on nature, no event lacks its religious interpretation, and no fact of life can be dismissed as accidental.

Hinduism is not much of a going-to-church religion. While Judaism and most sects of Christianity emphasize the idea of community or congregation—of believers gathered together—Hinduism speaks almost entirely to the individual, providing prayers and exercises to help the believer gain salvation. Many of India's modern leaders have blamed the country's disharmony in part on Hinduism's powerful emphasis on the individual. Good Hindus visit a temple every day if possible, though they may go at any time. Tem-

The ghats, or steps, of Benares, where the dead are cremated before their ashes are thrown into the river (Photo courtesy of Government of India Tourist Board)

ples are constructed for solitary worship. The supplicant stands at the threshold of a narrow, dark sanctuary, recites prayers to the idol secreted within, casting petals at its base and smudging its forehead with sandal paste, rings a bell that dangles above, and departs. The temple may be located on an island in the busiest crossroads of town; worshipers stop by in the midst of their own busy day, and the prayer flows into the rest of their daily activities. Religion does not stand

to the side of daily life but rather explains everything about it.

Food, for example, has religious meaning to the Hindu. Food is divided, according to the way it supposedly affects the eater, into *sattvas*, which is light and spiritual; *rajas*, which is passionate and energetic; and *tamas*, which represents heaviness, stupidity, uncleanness. All meat is *tamas*, so Hindus practice vegetarianism (though most are too poor to afford meat in any case) and consider meat-eaters spiritually impure. Hindus, even westernized ones, often explain diseases by claiming that sick people have "too much body heat" because of their diets. Food can also be distinguished according to its purity, or how likely it supposedly is to be polluted. Water is highly impure, and cooked food generally is less pure than uncooked food, which is in turn divided into various degrees of purity. This helps explain why members of high castes will not accept water or certain foods from members of low castes, and why wells have traditionally been off limits to Untouchables.

The importance of physical purity to a Hindu makes bathing a holy activity. The morning bath is a religious responsibility. The terrible notion of untouchability springs from the belief that people whose profession forces them into contact with unclean substances—such as sweepers, who dispose of human waste, and tanners, who bury or use animal carcasses—are themselves unclean. Orthodox high-caste individuals must immediately bathe to regain their purity if they accidentally take food from an Untouchable or draw water from a well used by one or even touch such a person in any way at all. Hindus consider certain rivers holy, especially the Ganges and the Brahmaputra, which rise in the Himalayas, supposed abode of Siva. A dip in either of these rivers, especially the Ganges, enjoys a special spiritual status, and Hindus will travel hundreds of miles to reach them. To have one's ashes scattered in the Ganges confers great spiritual blessings; in the ancient holy city of Benares, by the side of the Ganges, thousands of aging Indians await their death. And despite the filth that clogs the river, many Brahmans drink a glass of Ganges water every morning.

Hindus, then, do not exactly "practice" their religion as Catholics or Jews or Episcopalians do; they live their daily lives and observe the ancient rules of their culture. By satisfying all the obligations of caste, by hearing and reciting the tales of the gods, by their choice of food and even dress Hindus affirm their faith. Hinduism has no sacraments, no weekly religious services, not even a definite view of God. Hindus can believe in many gods, three gods, one god, or, like Nehru, no gods at all, and still remain Hindus. Gandhi felt that Hindus could adopt practically any belief, as long as they never swerved from one central goal: "Search after truth through nonviolent means." Leaving aside nonviolence, a Gandhian rather than a traditional approach, Hinduism becomes "the search for truth." This is obviously not a very useful definition, but it does help make it clear that Hinduism tolerates a wide variety of ideas.

Still, certain beliefs have remained with Hinduism from early times. Self-sacrifice, a practice common to many religions, occupies an especially important place in Hinduism. In Christianity self-sacrifice is basically charitable—good people place the needy before themselves. Hinduism, however, views self-sacrifice as a way of gaining purity; it is something you do for yourself, not for others. Just as good Hindus abstain from meat in order to safeguard the purity of their spirits, so they must learn not to care about the things of this world—money, power, even friendship—because such things prevent them from being free. When you want a thing deeply you are not really in control of yourself; you are guided by the desire. Self-sacrifice—doing away with everything you desire—makes true self-control possible. Yoga, which has become so popular in the United States, provides a set of exercises for the body and the mind with the goal of mastering physical reactions as well as thoughts. The true yogi is thus invulnerable to strong feelings. Krishna has such a person in mind when he says, in the *Bhagavad Gita*, a philosophical poem that comes near the end of the *Mahabharata*, "He who is without affection on any side, who does not rejoice or loathe as he obtains good or evil, his intelligence is firmly set. . . ."

One would think, in view of this philosophy, that Hinduism, like Buddhism, would be a religion of monks, totally withdrawn from the world. The image of the long-bearded sage confined to a mountain cave has always fascinated Hindus, but the caste system, after all, depends on everyone doing a job and not wandering off into the woods to seek truth. And, in fact, Krishna's speech caps a long argument in which he persuades Arjuna, a Kshatriya, to do his job—lead his soldiers into war, even against his own relatives. Arjuna feels pity, but Krishna tells him, first, that every man must satisfy his caste dharma and, second, that the wise man performs his duty without caring about what may result. Arjuna may gain a kingdom, but he must not become attached to power. A man can amass great wealth, but he must feel no concern about money. A husband and wife can enjoy sex, but they must not lose themselves in passion. Self-sacrifice needn't involve giving anything away, so long as people demonstrate indifference to the things that they have.

Though Hinduism is often spoken of as a "mystical" faith, its practical side is clear enough: it permits people to gain salvation without abandoning their work or their place in life. Yet Krishna's doctrine probably also leads to the nonchalance and detachment about life's tasks that both outsiders and Indian reformers often find frustrating. While America's Protestant work ethic demands a passionate involvement in the business of daily life, the Hindu ethic requires that individuals stand apart from their work, their minds elsewhere; a great source of calm, but not much of a goad to achievement.

Hindus believe neither in a hell nor in a heaven that we would recognize. Instead of an afterlife Hindu philosophy speaks of what is called the "transmigration of souls." After

death the body is destroyed—Hindus practice cremation—
thus freeing the soul to return to the world of spirit from
which it came. After a time it is reborn in a new form, higher
or lower on the caste scale depending on the person's actions
in the previous life—the law of karma. One seeks to climb
higher and higher from the world of plants to animals
through the various ranks of the caste ladder. Finally the
"achieved soul" is released from the endless cycle of birth,
death, and rebirth, and becomes part of the pure world of
spirit. This process may continue for thousands or even millions of years. According to the ancient scriptures we live in
the midst of a million-year period called *Kali Yuga*, the age
of death. Four such ages, beginning with the era of paradise
and ending with the era of death, make up a *mahayuga;* one
thousand *mahayugas* constitute only a single day in the life
of Brahma, whose life thus proceeds in 43-billion-year units.
It's no wonder that Hindus are famous for their patience.

Hinduism, then, requires its adherents to follow the path
of work and duty, but it does not really value the world; it
keeps society going, but it offers little encouragement to
someone inclined to change it. Buddhists, as we mentioned
earlier, believe that life is pain, but Hindus, though most
suffer more than enough, do not. Their epics are filled with
the bounty and beauty of life, their gods include practical
jokers and romancers; during one of the principal festivals,
Holi, celebrants forgive one another the sins of the past year
by plastering each other with paint and colored powder. To
the Hindu philosopher life is insignificant and unreal, rather
than agonizing. If this life is but a single link in an endless
chain of lives, and if our eighty years are but an infinitesimal
fraction of a single day in the timeless life of the gods, we
must think of ourselves as mere dots in the universe. Sometimes all of life is explained as a comedy that Brahma has
rigged up for his own enjoyment. Our eyes and our ears fool

us into thinking that the world is real. The word *maya* means both "the physical world" and "illusion." Wise people realize the emptiness of all their desires, so that they resemble the yogi who walks on burning coals and yet feels no pain: in the midst of his experiences his mind carries him away to a calm and quiet place.

II *Islam*

India's 85 million Muslims make it the second largest Islamic nation in the world (after Bangladesh), though they are vastly outnumbered by the country's 580 million Hindus. Outside Kashmir, the relatively small state in the Himalayas, Muslims don't predominate anywhere, scattered as they are throughout the north, which their ancestors conquered. Since their beliefs do not differ profoundly from those of Muslims elsewhere, we need not describe their religion in depth. More important is to explain why Islam has proved so incompatible with Hinduism and why the people of the two faiths have proved so reluctant to accept one another.

Much of the friction between the two peoples has little to do with religion. On the one hand, Hindus often accuse Muslims of pledging their loyalty to Pakistan rather than to India and of exacerbating the population problem by producing large families. Muslims, on the other hand, regard Hindus as arrogant, just as the Hindus regarded the British, and Muslims feel shut out of education, jobs, and political power. But two religions can hardly have less in common than Islam, which grew out of Judaism and Christianity, and Hinduism, which rose in the splendid isolation of India.

Islam draws no distinction between believers; many low-caste Hindus, attracted by a faith in which "all men can be kings," converted and took the name Khan, or "king." Muslims divide the world instead between "the faithful" and "heretics," with the latter more often cut to ribbons than converted. While Islam is democratic within the faith and intolerant without, Hinduism places every kind of barrier between its own members and absorbs rather than crushes outsiders. Everyone is included within the caste system, even outsiders. Non-Hindus are relegated to the same low status as Untouchables and are referred to as *mlechchas,* or "barbarians." Hinduism thus includes Muslims by assigning them the most humiliating possible position in the social order. Muslims, with their own ferocity toward nonmembers, often complain bitterly of the Hindu attitude of superiority.

While a Hindu can believe almost anything and remain a Hindu, Islam, a young religion by most standards, enforces strict beliefs about God, prayer, and morality. Hinduism lets individuals go their way—Gandhi, we recall, described the religion as a "search for truth"—whereas Islam tries to bind all its members together into a tightly knit group, as if it were an army. No idea of God falls outside of Hinduism, but Muslims chant, "There is no God but Allah." All Muslims must put down whatever they are doing in order to pray at five prescribed' times during the day, gathering together in the mosque for the evening prayer. Hinduism encourages detachment; Islam, passion. Hinduism may be the world's most casual religion; Islam, the least.

Whether it is because of these differences in temperament and doctrine, or because of hostility over power and prosperity, or because of a generalized sense of frustration looking for any outlet, Hindu-Muslim riots have become common since independence. Most occur in large, northern cities, where Muslims live in large numbers. These riots can be prompted by the most trivial event—a Muslim boy accidently draws a trickle of blood from a cow, which Hindus worship, while pushing it out of a shop—or by an unfounded rumor that pigs have been permitted to defile a mosque. In Moradabad, an industrial city in northern Uttar Pradesh, 142 people were killed in religious violence in August 1980; the violence spread as far as Kashmir before it was forcibly halted. Such violence is generally abetted by an anti-Muslim paramilitary group known as the R.S.S., whose members practice military maneuvers that they are accused of putting into effect during times of religious violence. India has lived with its religious problem for over five hundred years now without either solving it or being dissolved by it, and neither outcome seems likely for the near future.

III. Sikhism

India's most junior religion, Sikhism, sprang to life a scant five hundred years ago in the fertile climate of Punjab. Its founder, Guru Nanak, was a Kshatriya disgusted with the superstition and ritual of Hinduism; a background similar to Buddha's and Mahavira's. When Guru Nanak went to Benares he waded into the sacred Ganges, where Hindus were splashing water eastward, according to religious custom, in order to nourish the rising sun. Guru Nanak promptly began splashing water in the opposite direction. When a member of the baffled crowd asked why he was facing backward, he replied that his fields lay to the west, in Punjab, and he had as good a chance of irrigating them by splashing water from the Ganges as the others did of feeding the sun. Nanak, like Buddha before him and Vivekenanda after him, thought of himself not as the founder of a new religion but as a reformer bringing reason and simplicity to a religion corrupted by age.

But Nanak appointed a successor, the teachings of the

gurus began forming themselves into a scripture, and the gurus' followers began thinking of themselves as members of a new faith. Sikhs rejected the caste system and many of the popular Hindu customs, but during its first century Sikhism remained more or less a reform version of Hinduism. At that point Sikhism might easily enough have subsided back into Hinduism (it still may—Buddhism took 1,200 years to be swallowed), but the Moghuls, with their fierce intolerance of nonbelievers, tried to wipe the faith out instead of waiting for the enthusiasm to die down. Akbar naturally got on well with the Sikhs, inviting them to his religious conferences, but Jahangir captured the fifth guru, Arjun, and apparently had him dumped into the Jumna river. Arjun's son, Hargobind, "strapped on the sword"—in fact he strapped one on either side—and called on his fellow Sikhs to face martyrdom in defense of the faith, fighting the Muslims with their own militarism. From this moment on Sikhs became a military caste as well as members of a religion, fighting against Muslims and British for their independence and serving in the Indian army in large numbers, even in the present day.

The gurus who followed Hargobind concerned themselves with matters of war as much as faith. But the tenth and final guru, Gobind Singh, laid down the rules by which Sikhs now conduct themselves. He forbade the use of tobacco and liquor, prohibited sexual intercourse with Muslims, compiled hymns into scriptures, and drew up the "five symbols" by which Sikhs are now identified. A Sikh must never cut his hair (a practice adopted from Hindu holy men), instead wearing it tied up inside a turban; he must carry a comb and wear a steel wrist guard, a sword, and short pants. The last two have been mostly discarded by now, but the other three symbols remain.

With no male heirs to follow him as guru, Gobind Singh made an extraordinary decision: he appointed the scriptures

themselves, known as the *granths*, to succeed him as guru. In few other religions does the reading of scripture enjoy such prominence; the Sikhs acknowledge no other authority save the granths. In a Sikh temple, or *gurdwara*, the granths are raised on a covered pedestal, with a reader sitting behind in order to read the particular prayer or hymn that the worshiper wishes to hear. (Many Sikhs cannot read the old script in which the granths are written.) Good Sikhs are

The Golden Temple in Amritsar, spiritual center of Sikhism (Photo courtesy of Government of India Tourist Board)

expected to read the granths, or hear them read, every morning, and repeat to themselves the name of God—*Waheguru*, or "Wonderful lord."

Much of the doctrine of Sikhism sounds like that of Hinduism, in part because the early gurus thought of themselves as reform Hindus. The granths speak of God as "all-pervading"—that is, as a substance that is everywhere at once, rather than as a person in heaven. Brahma, Siva, and

Vishnu are the creations of this God. Sikh philosophy speaks of rebirth into a higher status, until finally the soul is merged with God. Sikhs celebrate a number of Hindu festivals.

But where Hinduism preaches a cool sense of detachment from the world, Sikhism not only permits but requires its members to involve themselves with their own work and that of their fellow men. Faith never stands in the way of action. "When you wish to embark on an undertaking," wrote Guru Hargobind, "pray about it and then get on with it." Sikhism has no place for the monk, reserving its respect for the *grihastha*, or householder. Sikhs are great builders of hospitals, schools, and charitable institutions. The gurdwara is often surrounded by a school, a communal kitchen, a clinic, a rest station.

Sikhs shatter the common image of Indians as a frail, philosophical, stoical people defeated by their difficult surroundings. Sikh men and women are tall and solidly built. The men are trained in military and athletic skills from an early age. While most Indians prefer to stay near home, Sikhs have migrated throughout India as well as the United States and Canada. As farmers and businessmen they have proved immensely successful, in part because of their willingness to take risks. Sikhs often become taxi drivers out of an unwillingness to work for an employer. Outside of Punjab they stick together in tight communities.

Total religious tolerance, respect for others' gods, is a cardinal tenet of Sikhism alone among the native faiths of India. If anything Sikhs have recently become more casual about their own faith, more worldly, than most other Indians. But this nonchalance has led, inevitably, to a movement in the opposite direction. As Islamic fundamentalism has become a force throughout the Arab world, so Sikh fundamentalism has risen in Punjab. And as with Islamic fundamentalism, a deep religious impulse has been combined with a deep nationalistic one to produce a powerful and dangerous political movement. Beginning about 1980, Sikh politicians banded with radical preachers to demand greater rights for Sikhs and for Punjab. This movement, which we will discuss at length later on, eventually led to a frightening campaign of terrorism and finally to the bloodiest internal battle in the history of free India. The military problem has been solved, at least temporarily, but the Sikhs remain angry and alienated. And after many generations of living in harmony with Hindu India, the Sikhs are now feared, distrusted, and even hated.

IV Buddhism, Jainism, Christianity, and Zoroastrianism

Buddhism and Jainism are India's two other home-grown religions; Christianity and Zoroastrianism, its two other imported ones. Both Buddhists and Jains, we saw, were mostly absorbed back into Hinduism over a thousand years ago. Jain monks are periodically seen in the streets of India. The most orthodox go entirely naked, and their passage through a town invariably draws a crowd of gaping citizens, with mothers doing their best to herd their children inside. Most of the three million nonmonastic Jains live in cities, engage in business, and practice a faith not distinct from Hinduism.

Buddhists remain in slightly larger numbers. As Buddhism passed away from India it migrated both north and east; today most of India's Buddhists live in the mountainous states of the north and resemble Mongolians and Tibetans more than Indians of the plains. In fact much of the community is composed of Tibetan Buddhists who fled their native land in the wake of the Chinese invasion of 1959. The Dalai Lama, Buddhism's high priest, has been living in exile in the mountain city of Dharamsala since that year. Though these Buddhists worship a number of Hindu gods, they practice a faith similar to the Buddhism practiced elsewhere in Asia.

India also has its freshly minted Buddhists. The greatest leader that the Untouchable community has yet produced, Dr. B. R. Ambedkar, helped lead India to independence, personally drew up much of the new nation's constitution, and sought in every way possible to promote the cause of the caste from which he had emerged. Ambedkar saw that the greatest obstruction confronting his people was their own acceptance of their place as dictated by Hinduism. Only by choosing a new religion could they abandon their lowly station. If they adopted Islam or Christianity they would make themselves foreigners in their own country; Buddhism had the advantage of being a native religion. Ambedkar's subsequent attempt to convert Untouchables to Buddhism succeeded only in his home state of Maharashtra, and there only partially. The Dalits, as his followers are called, worship Buddha, but are still regarded as Untouchables by Hindus. Their religion consists of Hinduism as much as Buddhism. Ambedkar has been elevated by these simple people into a god, and he is worshiped as much as Buddha. Dalit institutions give equal prominence to statues of the two figures, human and divine.

Christianity arrived on Indian shores, as legend has it, with the pilgrimage of Saint Thomas in A.D. 72. Missionary activity had to wait, however, until the arrival of the European explorers in the sixteenth century. The hardy Jesuits of France, Portugal, and England made it their policy to search out the most inaccessible corners of the continent, and today many of the eighteen million Christians in India can be found in the steep hills of Kerala and the distant tribal regions of the northeast. The high degree of literacy and English proficiency of the people of Kerala and the area's excellent rural medical facilities probably owe much to the long-standing presence of missionaries. Goa, a western port ruled by the Portuguese until the Indians kicked them out in 1961, remains a city of cathedrals and Catholics. Although Christians outnumber Sikhs, they are scattered geographically and have not formed significant political or cultural groups of their own; thus their impact on India is not especially great.

Zoroastrianism, on the other hand, has only 120,000 believers but enjoys influence far out of proportion to this tiny figure. Zoroaster lived and preached over three thousand years ago. His faith served as the state religion of ancient Persia until that country was overrun by Alexander. Zoroaster's remaining followers, expelled from their homeland in the seventh century, scattered themselves across Asia, as the Jews had done a thousand years before them. Those who traveled to India, now known as Parsis (meaning Persians), have kept the religion alive. The Parsis farmed the soil of western India until the English began establishing factories there. The English recognized that the Parsis saw themselves as outsiders, as religious exiles often do, and hired them as middlemen between themselves and their Indian employees. The Parsis were also shrewd traders and soon dominated much of the trade not controlled by Europeans. Parsi businessmen remained loyal to the British almost to the bitter end, supplying their troops with European goods. Parsis still see themselves as a people apart, wearing Western-style clothes and eating mild food. Parsis have maintained a large stake in shipping and trade and claim among their number India's second wealthiest family, the Tatas.

Zoroastrianism has much in common with Christianity and Judaism. Zoroastrians believe in one God and do not permit images to be made of him. Heaven, hell, and purgatory all figure in the *Zend-Avesta*, the Zoroastrian scripture. Both water and fire are sacred and are not to be polluted.

Prayers are performed facing a flame, and nine fires must be lit, one from another, to refine the flame for a Zoroastrian temple. Zoroastrians, like Hindus, do their praying privately, in special rooms set aside for that purpose in every household.

Parsis have been divided by two strong impulses. Like the Jews, they have been tempted to blend into their adopted home as they have grown wealthier and more secure. And yet, also like the Jews as well as the Sikhs, their strong sense of cultural pride has helped them maintain their culture despite their small numbers and their long stay in India. Parsis are justly famous for their philanthropy, but their first concern has always been their own people. Parsis have built hospitals, retirement homes, and other welfare insititutions to ensure their own prosperity and to serve Indians generally. This sense of community—of owing your first loyalty to others of your faith—seems to be the key to a religion's survival in India. So pervasive is the caste system, and so flexible and indistinct are Hinduism's religious principles, that a rival faith is hard pressed to skirt their boundaries. Hinduism's weakness, perhaps, is its sense of individualism: it is hard to imagine a Hindu crusade (though it is easy to imagine a Hindu riot). Religions that promote a strong sense of togetherness have prospered in the Hindu nation.

5
Democracy and Nation Building

Democracy has not proved very popular among the world's poor nations, especially the new ones. In all of South America, whose nations have recently been repudiating military dictators, only Venezuela carries on an unbroken tradition of civilian rule. With only a few exceptions African nations are ruled by members of the dominant tribe, with one man frequently enjoying almost absolute power. A large number of noncommunist countries in Asia are ruled sternly, if efficiently, by dictators, military or civilian, with the help of a tiny number of wealthy businessmen. Many of these officially democratic states are less democratic than the communist ones. Almost alone among all these nations India can boast an authentic, if slightly shaky, democracy. The large and fairly powerful military has no role whatever in Indian politics. Although one caste, the Brahmans, has held most of the important positions despite its tiny numbers, other castes have gained an increasingly large share of power. And although Indians have had only since 1947 to shift their traditional loyalties from one of the old warring states or principalities to a single nation, a civil war or a revolution has yet to occur.

Many people argue that a poor country will do better with a "benevolent despot"—an all-powerful individual dedicated to progress—than with democratic governments that are too busy settling arguments to bring about essential sweeping changes. India's three and a half decades of democracy have not ended poverty, after all; and, though both a revolution and a civil war have been avoided, violence between disgruntled groups has grown ever worse. Is India's democracy a success or a failure? Is it really a democracy at all? These questions go to the heart of our judgment not only of India but of the other nations that have tried different solutions to similar problems. In the next two chapters we will seek to answer these questions.

I The Constitution

In 1947 when India's new rulers began drawing up a constitution, they looked to both Britain and the United States for guidance. Britain had been the enemy, but it had also been, unwittingly, the teacher of democratic principles. The United States, of course, stood as an example of another nation that had liberated itself from British tyranny by means of a popular uprising. The United States had another lesson to offer: too vast and too varied to be governed from a single place, it had established a federal system whereby many important decisions were left to state and local governments.

India, like England, is governed by a prime minister elected by members of the ruling party. The constitution also gives great powers to a president, who appoints the prime minister, cabinet members, and judges of the supreme court and other high courts and who must sign all bills into law. But the president has in fact been little more than a figurehead since Nehru, as prime minister, began trespassing on the powers of the office in 1950. The Parliament runs more on the English than the American model: the lower house, called the Lok Sabha (People's House, or House of Commons), is elected directly by the people and controls almost all of the legislative power; the upper house, called the Rajya Sabha (Royal House, or House of Lords), is elected by the state assemblies (as our own Senate was until 1911), is heavily populated with nonpolitical celebrities, and has little real authority. The judicial system moves upward in a scale from local courts to state-level courts to the high courts, which resemble our federal district courts, to the supreme court.

Indian lawmakers benefited from American experience by including in the long list of fundamental rights not only the protections afforded by our Bill of Rights but others included in later amendments. The fundamental rights, which cannot be taken away by federal or state law, include freedom of speech, assembly, and religion (though not press); the right to buy, hold, and sell property; the right to equal protection before the law; freedom from discrimination based on religion, race, caste, sex, or place of birth; and the right to equal opportunity in employment.

A special concern of the constitution's creators, constantly reiterated by national leaders since then, was the creation of a secular state—not a nonreligious state but one in which no religion or caste would enjoy official, favored status. Freedom from discrimination, for example, includes the right of access to "wells, tanks, bathing ghats, roads," and public places maintained by the state—places that otherwise might be off limits to the low castes. Another article specifically abolishes untouchability. But laws have a hard time overcoming tradition: untouchability and the caste system in general remain strong today.

But the authors of the constitution considered this list of protections inadequate. These strictures told the government, by and large, what it could not do, but the authors thought that the constitution should also spell out what the government ought to do. With this in mind they included the Directive Principles of State Policy in the document. These principles had no legal force, but they stood as a statement of purpose, somewhat like the Preamble to the U.S. Constitution. Among the goals set out by the Directive Principles were the creation of adequate jobs for all citizens; the distribution of wealth and power for the good of all, and thus the avoidance of great wealth; and the promotion of the interests of Untouchables, now called Scheduled Castes.

The Directive Principles were not supposed to conflict with fundamental rights. However, the individual's right to hold on to his property clashes with the state's responsibility to avoid unfair concentrations of wealth, especially in a country where great wealth exists amid great poverty. In all nations, but especially in poor ones, the needs of the people as a whole will always come into conflict with the rights of individuals: the right of a businessman to build a factory, for example, versus the need of a community to keep its trees and streams and clean air. India is unusual only in embedding this dilemma in its constitution. The conflict has persisted since independence, and fundamental rights, which generally require that the government do nothing, have often won out over the Directive Principles, which demand that the government do something.

The new government held few illusions about national loyalty. The English had done nothing to prevent India from splitting into dozens of states and literally hundreds of

pocket principalities. The idea of Hindustan—one nation—
had remained only a vague glimmer until independence.
India's deep divisions were not abolished when it became an
independent nation. Trying to rule this vast hodgepodge
from Delhi alone would have been folly, and in any case
Gandhi's followers preferred the idea of many small governments to that of one huge one. Thus the creators of the
constitution looked to America when they established the
new federal system. Dr. Ambedkar, who had studied law at
Columbia University, even wrote of "the United States of
India," though this name was later scrapped.

In the final draft of the constitution a large cluster of powers was reserved for the states; these include police power,
education, justice, control of local governments, and almost
all decisions relating to agriculture. States have often proved
more conservative than the central government and have
used their powers to frustrate attempts at change; this distribution of power, however, has probably helped keep India a
stable nation, since no state or group within a state has felt
entirely locked out of power.

II The Great Experiment: Nehru and One-party Democracy

The role of politics in a democratic society is to organize
competing groups—rich and poor, farmer and worker, northerner and southerner—so that all voices can be heard and so
that each group is willing to work with the others when
decisions have to be made. Democracy, in other words, permits conflict in hope that it will lead to cooperation. In developing countries the emphasis often falls on compelling
cooperation rather than attaining it through open conflict:
authoritarian rulers of such countries generally claim that if
all citizens were permitted their say people would refuse to

abide by the rules of democracy and the nation would become ungovernable. In such nations, either people have such faith in their leaders that they willingly forget their own interests, which is rare, or they are compelled to cooperate, usually by means of threats and occasional displays of police power.

India, unlike other new nations, has generally sought to create cooperation by permitting conflict. As we trace India's recent political history we will see that the young country achieved this delicate balance through its unique system of one-party democracy. As the one-party system went into an inevitable decline after the death of Nehru, the balance of cooperation and conflict began also to deteriorate. Conflict in India has grown increasingly disorganized, cooperation has been forced rather than freely given, and the nation has stumbled into a wilderness of confusion.

By the time the English left India in 1947, the Congress had already been running much of the local government for more than twenty-five years; thus the English decision to hand over power to the Congress, which was under the leadership of Nehru, was the natural one. At the time the Congress was not a political party, though its members had contested state and local elections, but a revolutionary organization. With the goal of liberating India from the English, the Congress had forged unity from the widest possible variety of people: businessmen and socialists, intellectuals and peasants, Hindus and, to some extent, Muslims. But once these people had succeeded in their common task—achieving independence—they were ready to start thinking about their own particular interests. The Congress Socialist Party, for example, split from the Congress in 1934, came back to the fold in 1939 to provide unity against the English, and then, after independence, immediately began agitating once more against the conservative members of Congress.

The responsibility of preventing India from falling apart fell squarely on the shoulders of the new prime minister, Nehru. History, fortunately, could not have chosen a more appropriate man for the job. The Indian people venerated Nehru not only as the leader of the liberation forces, who had suffered through nine years in dismal English prisons, but also as the son of Motilal Nehru, who had led the Congress in the 1920s; Nehru thus inherited his power, like one of the princes of old. Despite his English education and Western manners, Nehru felt a deep, if somewhat vague, bond with the common people, and they in turn thought of him as a great man who could deal with foreigners on their own terms, without ever forgetting his own people. Finally, Nehru's abiding, almost religious belief in the destiny of his young nation led him to do whatever he thought was necessary to preserve its unity. At times he sacrificed his own beliefs—about the economy, for example—when he felt that advancing them would cause deep division in the government. Nehru has been criticized for failing to pursue many of his own goals, but because he prized democracy and national unity above all else, he was never untrue to himself.

When he assumed the prime ministership Nehru had to decide what to do with the Congress. Gandhi and his followers wished to dismantle it as the first step in creating a "partyless democracy." Gandhi's revolution, we recall, had always been a moral one, aimed at brotherhood and harmony; political parties, pitting one set of interests against another, would make those goals unattainable. Instead Gandhi advocated a government by consensus, in which all would agree on a common notion of the national good. On the other side were those willing to split off and form new parties, thus plunging the Congress into full-scale political warfare. Nehru characteristically chose to navigate between the two sides; throughout his seventeen-year prime ministership he sought to keep the Congress broad enough so that it could contain almost all points of view, and yet he did little to prevent political competition, perhaps because there was little anyone could do to prevent it.

Nehru's Congress party was like India itself: divided and confused by every kind of disagreement, but united in one body nevertheless. India's leading social scientist, Rajni Kothari, has described his nation's greatest achievement as "building a unity which derived its strength from infinite diversity and differentiation and did not need to steamroller the country into some dead uniformity under a leader or a party or an idea." Socialists and capitalists were constantly at war within the party: the capitalists were in the ascendancy until the death of their leader, Sardar Patel, in 1950; the socialists, led by Nehru, carved out policy during most of the 1950s; and the capitalists again gained ground in the late 1950s and mid-1960s. At various times members of the two factions split off into separate parties, but Nehru usually managed, through skillful compromise, to keep them together in the Congress. We will see later, however, that this tactic did not work well in Nehru's absence.

III Other Parties

India had, in fact, a multitude of parties, but most represented a narrow cultural, regional, or political point of view. The Congress was the party of the whole nation: to join was to affirm your modern faith in the "all-India" idea, as opposed to an old-fashioned loyalty to a region or a group. The small, satellite parties, however, played a crucial role in en-

suring that the Congress-led government remained respon-
sive to local interests.

Some of these other parties have been organized around
political beliefs rather than local concerns. India has had a
large, tightly organized Communist party since the early
twentieth century. Its popularity has been limited by the
hostility of a religious people to an atheist system, but the
party has enjoyed perennial success in West Bengal and
Kerala. In 1964 the party split into the CPI and the
CPI(M)—"M" for "Marxist." In the late 1960s a Marxist-
Leninist group, the CPI(M-L) broke off from the CPI(M).
Many of its members were educated young people, disil-
lusioned with the democratic process, and for a time they
committed terrorist acts throughout northeast India. They
were finally subdued in a series of shootouts which shocked
the nation.

On the other side of the political spectrum stand the pro-
business parties. India has only had one important political
party of this kind, the Swatantra, whose principal concern
was promoting the interests of busines. The Swatantra
reached the height of its power when it won forty-two
seats—8 percent of the total—in the 1967 election. After a
bad thrashing in the 1971 election the party broke up into a
number of other conservative groups.

Of all the "cultural" parties that represent a particular
community or region or language, the largest and most con-
troversial is the Jana Sangh, a Hindu nationalist party that
advocates the use of Hindi as a national language as well as
such religious measures as the prohibition of cow slaughter.
Many Jana Sangh partisans are also members of the
Rashtriya Swayamesevak Sangh (RSS), the paramilitary
group mentioned earlier. The party itself has no official anti-
Muslim policy, but opponents believe that its existence
threatens India's secular state.

Most of India's parties have been not national but regional, expressing the concerns of religious, ethnic, or linguistic groups. The Akali Dal, in Punjab, has served as a vehicle for Sikh sentiment, while the state house of Tamil Nadu has been controlled for several years by an anti-Hindu, pro-southern party called the DMK and its opponent, the AIA-DMK. Indian politicians and political scientists disagree as to whether these parties are good, because they represent their members' passionate regional loyalty, or bad, because they breed hostility to the central government.

Throughout the 1950s these parties provided a strictly minor key to the Congress, but the one-party system began to weaken with the third national election, in 1962. The Congress won three-quarters of the seats—hardly a cause for discomfort—but for the first time major national parties contested the election from both the left and the right. The Swatantra gained eighteen seats and the CPI, twenty-nine. The Congress had begun to lose its ability to keep dissenters in the fold. Rifts within the Congress widened in 1963 when Nehru's ministers offered their resignations as part of what was called the Kamaraj Plan; among the few resignations that Nehru accepted were those of conservatives whose economic ideas did not match his own.

With Nehru's death, on May 27, 1964, power passed into the hands of five chief ministers known as the Syndicate. Wishing to maintain Congress dominance without a truly strong prime minister—who would, after all, eliminate their own power—the Syndicate settled on Lal Bahadur Shastri, a long-time Nehru loyalist whose views did not appear especially strong. Shastri managed to make himself popular by directing a victory, or at least a stalemate, over the Pakistanis in a 1965 border war, but he died of a heart attack while negotiating the peace the next year in Tashkent.

The Syndicate, still in the driver's seat, looked around

once more. No candidate seemed more appropriate than Nehru's daughter, Indira Gandhi, then the information and broadcasting minister. (Mrs. Gandhi's last name comes from her late husband, Feroze Gandhi, not from the Mahatma.) Mrs. Gandhi had ten years of government and party experience, she was a member of the great Nehru family (at her first swearing-in the audience roared, "Long live Jawaharlal Nehru!"), and she seemed likely to submit to the Syndicate's will. Mrs. Gandhi gained the prime ministership in 1966; but she proved a good deal feistier than was expected.

IV Indira Gandhi and the End of Stability

By 1969, far from being submissive, Mrs. Gandhi had presided over the end of her father's experiment in govern-

Prime Minister Indira Gandhi (Photo courtesy of the Indian Embassy to the United States)

ment by compromise. In 1966 she formed her cabinet after
lengthy consultations with other Congress leaders. By the
next year, when she felt more sure of herself, she submitted
her new cabinet to Parliament after consulting only a single
adviser—behavior that her father, who sought to include
others in his deliberations, would have found shocking. In a
shift of favor she restored to the cabinet in 1967 Morarji
Desai, an associate of Gandhi's and a leader of the conservatives. Then she disposed of him after another change of
allegiance.

Without Nehru the Congress began to lose its special
status as the party of independence, the party above politics;
many congressmen saw that it might be to their advantage to
bolt to a new party. The 1967 national elections, India's
fourth, proved something close to a disaster for the Congress. The party won only 284 seats, or 55 percent of the
total, while the Swatantra and the Jana Sangh won more
than twice as many votes as they had in 1962. The one-party
system was finished. Some MLAs, or state assemblymen,
sold their loyalty to the highest bidder; others were beaten
or terrorized into submission. In many states no single party
had been able to gain a majority, and governments rose and
fell. The machinery of government ground to a halt as state
parliaments witnessed scenes of chaos such as modern India
had never seen. A dispute between the governor and the
assembly speaker in Punjab led to a fracas, described by
Francine Frankel in *India's Political Economy, 1947–77*, in
which "several men jumped on to the speaker's rostrum and
grappled with the opposition members there. A hand to
hand fight followed and continued for a quarter of an hour
when the rostrum was cleared. . . . Amidst deafening noise
and thumping of tables and shouting of slogans, all the
financial business before the House . . . was reported and
completed under the Presidentship of the Deputy Speaker."

The political chaos was immediately translated into physical disorder in the country as a whole, as if India had been waiting for the opportunity to explode. Riots and organized violence broke out in West Bengal, Assam, Maharashtra, and elsewhere. Urban workers struck against employers, peasants against landlords. The guerillas of the CPI (M-L), known as the Naxalites, conducted a form of class warfare. Nehru's fears had been borne out: without a single party somehow holding together people with different beliefs and permitting them all free expression, the deep historical divisions of the country would cause politics to splinter and, in the nation at large, would turn one group against another.

The crippling blow to the era of consensus and compromise came in 1969, when Mrs. Gandhi decided to part ways with the Syndicate. The economy had been functioning badly, and Mrs. Gandhi, in 1967, had staked out a bold new program which linked her with the young socialists and set her against the older, conservative branch of the party led by the Syndicate. Tensions between the two groups finally blew up when each backed a different candidate for president. Mrs. Gandhi won after an all-out battle, and the infuriated Congress leadership expelled her from the party, even though she was prime minister. After eighty-five years of unity the Congress split in two, with the conservatives, led by Morarji Desai, calling themselves the Congress (O) and members of the two groups launching bitter personal attacks against one another. At that moment India's period of conflict, party-switching, cynicism, and confusion began.

Mrs. Gandhi could not be held entirely responsible for this era of strife. First of all, no one can succeed a hero and patriarch and hope to enjoy his undivided popularity, not even his daughter. Politicians like Morarji Desai, who had held their ambition in check during Nehru's lifetime, felt that they no longer had a responsibility to do so. Second, much of the conflict and violence that arose after 1967 owed their birth to conditions that Mrs. Gandhi inherited— poverty and deep anxiety over what one's neighbor might do. And third, while her father sometimes sacrificed bold programs in order to preserve a sense of unity, Mrs. Gandhi purposely did away with compromise in order to advance her new socialistic proposals—greatly increasing government control over banking, insurance, and the distribution of food. Mrs. Gandhi's loyalties shifted with the years, however, and instead of trying to embrace as many groups as possible, as her father did, she threw her hat in first with one side, then another.

Over the next six years Mrs. Gandhi consolidated her powers at the expense of party leaders, state governments, and even her own cabinet. The smashing victory that the Congress won in the 1971 national elections was widely interpreted as a personal triumph for Mrs. Gandhi; thus she could dispense with many of the allies, on both the left and right, whom she had needed after her shaky 1967 victory. And the prime minister brought more and more powers into her own office, taking personal control, in 1970, of the Home Ministry, which runs India's vast civil service, bringing India's version of the FBI, known as the CBI, into the cabinet, and greatly expanding the Research and Analysis Wing into something of a secret police force. By the mid-1970s Mrs. Gandhi enjoyed power far greater than her father had ever known; critics increasingly charged that she had cashed in Nehru's commitment to democracy for greater personal power.

And the country was not thriving. Mrs. Gandhi had magnificently promised to *garibi hatao*—abolish poverty— in the 1971 election, thus raising hopes that she could not possibly satisfy. As inflation soared in 1973, workers took to the streets to demonstrate against the government. Riots broke out in Ahmedabad, the capital of Gujarat, finally forcing the Congress-led state government to resign. Independence hero Jayaprakash Narayan organized massive strikes all over Bihar. Though he failed to bring the government down, the "J. P. movement" soon spread across India, recalling the civil disobedience campaign conducted against the British. Narayan and other national leaders called on Mrs. Gandhi to resign for the national good. When the Allahabad High Court decided that the prime minister had won her seat in the 1971 election through unfair means and stripped her of her right to vote in Parliament, the chorus calling for her resignation grew louder.

V *Emergency Powers—The Rise of Sanjay Gandhi*

Resignation would have been entirely out of character for Mrs. Gandhi, and instead she turned her guns on the enemy. On June 26, 1975, she informed a stunned nation that India's very stability, and not merely her own position, was jeopardized, a situation that could be handled only by the use of emergency powers offered by the constitution for times of national crisis. That same morning members of the police force fanned out across the country, arresting opposition leaders, including the venerated "J.P." himself. Power was cut off in the offices of Delhi newspapers. All constitutional protections, including fundamental rights, were suspended; the central government absorbed all powers from the states; and newspapers were rigorously censored. And like a thunderclap stilling a roomful of clamorous people, the Emergency spread a deathly silence across the continent.

The Emergency came to symbolize the complete breakdown of Nehru's India. Along with the other leaders of the young nation, Nehru had tried to weave India's many threads into a single fabric through the patient and trying exercise of consultation and compromise. Through the force of his own personality Nehru had given his people a sense of being a part of a proud experiment in nationhood. Now the dialogue among India's many competing groups had turned to a shouting match, and that, in turn, had been crushed. India had always fascinated the world as the unlikeliest member of the club of democratic nations; now it seemed to have dropped out of the club.

During the Emergency Mrs. Gandhi turned more and more to her son Sanjay, until then a failed businessman who had promised to manufacture a "people's car" for only $1,200 and had proved unable to produce a single commercial vehicle even at a cost of $6,000. Sanjay toured the country with his mother's indefatigable energy, pressing her twenty-point program and his own four-point program with such simple slogans as "Work more, talk less" and "Each one teach one." Sanjay's power was well known, and he was feared and flattered. When he joined the Youth Congress, millions of others joined. When he arrived at an airport, every official of the state came to greet him. He undertook great campaigns of "progress." His slum clearance program not only cleared slums but displaced thousands of the urban poor from their homes; his family planning program succeeded in sterilizing an estimated 9 million men, but they included young boys, old men, and defenseless villagers dragged off buses. Sanjay helped his friends and punished his enemies, creating a sense of terror among senior politicians, businessmen, and government employees.

Mrs. Gandhi had probably intended the Emergency as a temporary move, but she permitted it to drag on, perhaps because she found the new clean, efficient, and silent India a good deal easier to govern than its noisy predecessor. Sanjay, who had remarked that "future generations will remember us not by how many elections we had, but by how much progress we made," was content to extend the Emergency indefinitely. But Mrs. Gandhi had inherited a democratic nation, and by the end of 1976 she had apparently grown uncomfortable with her dictatorship. Taking the lack of criticism as a sign of her popularity, she released the political prisoners at the end of January and, lifting the Emergency, scheduled elections for March.

The results astonished everyone, Mrs. Gandhi most of all. The opposition had barely six weeks to recover from their jailing and conduct a nationwide campaign. With the four principal opposition parties fighting as one and with defectors streaming out of the Congress, the new Janata party won a devastating victory, winning almost every seat in the north, defeating Mrs. Gandhi and Sanjay decisively in their own constituencies. Mrs. Gandhi had gravely underestimated the unpopularity of the Emergency and, perhaps, the depth of the hatred people felt toward her son. India had shown that it valued its brief experience of democracy too much to discard it.

VI *Janata Interlude*

Once the excitement over the restoration of democracy died down, the Janata found itself facing the same problem that had driven Mrs. Gandhi to declare the Emergency: how to bring about order in an increasingly dissatisfied, disordered nation. But the Janata had promised liberty, and the nation planned to enjoy its new-found freedom. The frustration which had found no outlet during the Emergency burst forth with the victory of the Janata: factory workers went on strike, students demonstrated and halted classes, anti-Muslim Hindus resumed their agitation. Janata Prime Minister Morarji Desai was determined to rule as a democrat, and shared his mentor Gandhi's horror of police

methods. The daily breakdown to which India is so prone—
trains running late, power failures, food scarcity, bureaucrats
refusing to take responsibility—seemed to become more and
more pervasive. Mrs. Gandhi's efficient authoritarianism began to look almost attractive next to the Janata's hapless
democracy.

The members of the new coalition, who had nothing in

Indira Gandhi addressing an election rally near Calcutta (Photo courtesy of AP/Wide World)

common save dislike for Mrs. Gandhi, began to connive against one another. The government almost ceased functioning. In July 1979 finance minister Charan Singh finally succeeded in toppling his own prime minister. Yet another election was declared, with Singh appointed as the "caretaker" prime minister.

Mrs. Gandhi's humiliating defeat had appeared to put a

full stop to her political career, but the Janata's disarray had made her brand of discipline more attractive. In 1978 she boldly recaptured the Congress by splitting it in two once again and heading up the Congress (I)—"I" for "Indira." And now Mrs. Gandhi was to benefit from the political disintegration she had helped bring about. In the 1980 election party attachment became meaningless, with politicians scurrying back and forth from one party to another in a frantic effort to be on the winning side.

The election appeared to many Indians to display politics as a meaningless and cynical pursuit of power. Mrs. Gandhi, with her scaled-down promise of "a government that works," won a victory as astonishing as her previous defeat, gaining two-thirds of the seats. We can ransack modern history without finding an example of a political comeback as bold and as supremely successful as Mrs. Gandhi's.

VII Indira Gandhi: Triumph and Tragedy

Indira Gandhi's return to power began with her son Sanjay's violent death and ended, four and a half years later, with her own. For several months after the election it seemed clear that she was preparing to hand the daily direction of the government to Sanjay, an exceedingly shrewd politician but a divisive leader who inspired fervent loyalty and deep loathing in apparently equal parts. But Sanjay's death in a plane crash in June 1980 left his mother not only deeply bereaved but uncertain where to turn. She turned, inevitably, to her own family, to the family that had dominated India with few intervals for over sixty years. At the time of Sanjay's death her younger son, Rajiv, was living quietly as an airline pilot, keeping a careful distance from politics. But Rajiv could not resist his mother's call to take an active part in Congress affairs, and soon he had become her heir apparent.

Over the course of the next few years the internal divisions that had plagued India grew worse and worse. Mrs. Gandhi seemed unable or unwilling to reach a compromise with unhappy groups around the country. Throughout 1982 long-time natives of the northeastern state of Assam agitated to have recent immigrants from Bangladesh, almost all of them Muslim, removed from the electoral rolls. In the spring of the next year the central government, unable to come to terms with the protestors, decided to go ahead with a planned election. Mrs. Gandhi's critics, frightened at the possibility of violence, urged her to postpone the polling, but without success. As the election started, killing broke out, between tribal and nontribal, immigrant and native, Hindu and Muslim. Each day's newspaper carried yet more horrible tales of whole villages slaughtered while police officials stood helplessly by. By the time the army moved in, days too late, several thousand Assamese had been murdered—the most violent riot in the history of modern India. The nation seemed to have hit bottom; but the worst was yet to come.

Soon after Mrs. Gandhi retook office several leaders of the Akali Dal, as well as other Sikh-dominated groups, began claiming that the Sikhs, and Punjabis in general, had been neglected and even oppressed by the central government. They demanded, among other things, special rights of self-rule for Punjab, a larger share of the river water that ran through the state, and special permission for Sikhs to carry their *kirpans*, or ceremonial swords, aboard planes. Mrs. Gandhi at first ignored these requests, then, as the campaign took the form of strikes and demonstrations, tried unsuccessfully to negotiate. As the more moderate Sikh leaders proved unable to wrest any major concessions from the government, radicals began to take over the movement. Both sides hardened their positions; occasional attempts at negotiation failed. By 1983 the Sikh agitation had taken the form of terrorism against Hindus and even moderate Sikhs; hit-and-run murders committed by masked men became daily events.

Meanwhile, the mastermind of the terrorist activity, a Sikh holy man named Sant Jarnail Singh Bhindranwale, holed up in the holiest of Sikh shrines, the Golden Temple, in Amritsar. There he and a growing band of followers began stockpiling arms, vowing to hold out against any government assault. The Sant calculated correctly that Mrs. Gandhi would be reluctant to attack the temple, if only for fear of provoking other Sikhs. For months the government hesitated, apparently paralyzed. Then, on June 4, 1984, 4,000 government troops, under cover of mortar and grenade fire, rushed into the temple complex. The Sikh warriors, it turned out, were well entrenched, extremely well armed, and eager for a glorious death. In the bloodbath that followed over the next several days as many as 1,000 of the radicals and 200 of the soldiers were killed. The sacred water tank was full of blood; parts of the temple were utterly smashed, though the most sacred portion was left unharmed. And the harmony of Hindus and Sikhs, long unquestioned, was destroyed altogether. A whole new form of enmity had been added to India's growing list of divisions.

The Sikh radicals finally gained their revenge. As Mrs. Gandhi emerged from the front door of her home on the morning of October 30, two of her bodyguards, both Sikhs, turned on her and pumped upward of 20 bullets into her torso, killing her immediately. In the aftermath of the Golden Temple invasion Mrs. Gandhi had been advised to rid her security staff of Sikhs. She had refused, arguing that

Militant Sikhs on top of a tower of the Golden Temple of Amritsar before the attack by government troops in June 1984 (Photo courtesy of AP/Wide World)

the danger was less important than her public display of trust. So in some ways she was killed by her own courage, which had always been beyond question. But she was killed, also, by her unwillingness to compromise with her critics and by her decision to solve a political problem with military force.

The next act of the government seemed inevitable: the swearing in of forty-year-old Rajiv Gandhi as the new prime minister. Rajiv appealed for calm, but there was nothing he or, apparently, anyone else could do about what followed: attacks on Sikhs all over India. Hindus blamed all Sikhs, and not just the two gunmen, for the death of the woman many of them had worshiped during her 15 years of rule. Businesses and houses owned by Sikhs were sacked and burned. Sikh taxi drivers were surrounded by mobs and attacked. Trains began to roll into New Delhi station bearing the bodies of Sikhs murdered along the way—a replay of the violence of Partition. Mobs consisting largely of Untouchables destroyed entire neighborhoods, while gangs of criminals arrived in vans, swept up video-cassette recorders, refrigerators, and the like, and made their escape. Both police and local politicians were implicated in the violence. When the slaughter exhausted itself after three days, 500 people were said to have been killed in New Delhi alone.

All of India looked to its grieving and untested new leader for guidance. Rajiv surprised his critics by remaining steady and quelling the violence as best he could. Knowing that the first thing he would have to do was to consolidate his own power, Rajiv called for an election at the end of the year. He then weeded out from the party some of Sanjay's more notorious associates, as well as several of his mother's loyalists. Campaigning as tirelessly as his mother, though without her electrifying style—Rajiv is a careful, plodding speaker—he won the greatest electoral victory in Indian history, de-

After the assassination of his mother, Rajiv Gandhi was sworn in as Prime Minister of India on October 31, 1984, by President Zail Singh (Photo courtesy of AP/Wide World)

feating practically every opposition leader and winning four
seats out of every five.

Rajiv remains an unknown quantity. To most Indians he
represents all things modern—a secular outlook, an indifference to issues of "left" and "right," a fondness for computers
and other high technology. Indians hope that he will reform
politics by doing away with his mother's insistence on blind
loyalty, her constant intriguing, her apparent acceptance of
incompetence and corruption. They hope that he will stick
to his emphasis on efficiency and dedication, to getting the
job done, and thus move India, if not into the twenty-first
century, at least into the twentieth. But it is far from clear
whether Rajiv has either the strength of his mother, to master his enemies and remain in power, or the wisdom of his
grandfather, to trust in the democratic process and the virtue
of patience.

It would be hard to think of a developing nation that
exercises its freedoms with more abandon than India. The
freedom to criticize the government in the press or in public
meetings, the right to strike, the right to replace one set of
leaders with another at election time: none of these prerogatives seems likely to rust from disuse. Democracy in India is
a daily fact. But the growing frequency of violence and
heightened conflict between one group and another—of
which we will hear more in the next chapter—implies a
widespread sense of frustration with the political system.
Perhaps Rajiv's greatest challenge is to overcome this frustration, to restore the faith in the system that has been erod-
ing for almost twenty years.

VIII Democracy from the Bottom Up

In order to function as a true democracy a country needs
more than political parties and elected parliaments; it needs

popular involvement. The role of democracy is not only to represent the interests of all the people—a benevolent dictator could do as much—but to give people an opportunity to participate in the decisions that will shape their lives. For this reason it has often been said that in a country like India, where the great masses of people are too uneducated to form sophisticated political views and too poor to worry about much except their next meal, politics is a sport played by a tiny group of well-to-do urbanites, a profession for the politicians and party workers. Yet even as politicians have increasingly ignored the public in order to fight one another, Indians have become passionately concerned about their rights and have used the electoral system to express their anger.

But to understand Indian democracy we should focus not only on national but on local politics; its issues and leaders are far more familiar to the average villager. Unlike many other poor nations, India has a highly developed system of local and county-wide politics. Essential to the notion of "partyless democracy" of the Gandhians was the belief that villages should be permitted to govern themselves. Gandhi considered the panchayat, the traditional village-level government, a model democratic institution and the ideal foundation for the Indian political system. Only by making power flow up from the panchayats, rather than down from Delhi, Gandhi felt, could India achieve a workable democracy. From the beginning Nehru sought to increase the importance of panchayats by giving them, rather than government bureaucrats, power over funds used to develop the villages. The goal of *panchayati raj*—village rule—gained legal force in 1958, when the government instructed the states to set up the system of local elected leadership that now exists throughout India.

This local government system consists of three layers: the *panchayat*, which represents a village or small group of villages; the *panchayat samiti,* consisting of panchayat chiefs from perhaps one hundred villages; and the *zilla parishad,* bringing together the samiti leaders of an entire district, covering as many as ten million people. Almost all the funds to be spent for development purposes—building roads, establishing health clinics, digging irrigation trenches, and the like—are funneled through this system, thus reserving a great deal of power at the local level. The panchayat election has also become immensely important, since the whole system functions as a pyramid with the village on the bottom. Nowadays political parties will often sponsor rival candidates, whereas individuals used to run as independents. The elections are often fiercely contested, with slogans scrawled all over the walls of buildings, thus giving villagers a more intimate taste of politics than they get from national events.

Elections, however, often have little to do with democracy. Voting in India is a group decision, not an individual one. With rare exceptions, all members of a family will vote the same way; all the servants in a household will vote the way the most educated or influential servant instructs them to; and every member of a *jati,* or clan group (a subset of a caste), will cast his ballot for a single candidate. The parties are thus enabled to dispense with the democratic process of going to the people, instead seeking to gratify a handful of leaders through favors of one sort or another. And if all else fails, a candidate can always resort to "capturing" election booths by hiring thugs to steal the ballot papers, throw out those belonging to the opposition, and mark up several hundred extras for their employer. The police, who are always stretched thin at election time, can often be persuaded to look the other way.

Though panchayati raj represents a most imperfect form of democracy, it seems to be getting better rather than worse. At first almost all panchayat leaders came from the higher castes, thus frustrating the government's goal of increasing the power of the so-called Scheduled Castes ("scheduled" by the constitution for special assistance); the higher up one went in the system, the more likely were the representatives to be well-to-do, educated, and employed as professionals rather than farmers. This pattern has begun to shift, however; members of the low castes have begun to assert themselves and gain new political power. We mentioned earlier how changes within the village had begun to erase the traditional bond between low-caste laborers and their high-caste employers; one of the consequences of this change has been the willingness of the Scheduled Castes to take the risk of seeking political power (the risk, that is, of antagonizing the powerful).

What is perhaps most important in assessing the quality of Indian democracy is that average voters have become accustomed to having their opinions solicited and to expressing them. In the days of Nehru the villagers had very little choice: the Congress was the only national, as opposed to regional, party with a strong rural base, and the villagers voted for the Congress routinely. Now a wide variety of parties appeal for their votes, offering extravagant promises in exchange. The villagers have become involved in politics; they have come to prize their votes; and they have seen that they can remove leaders who fail them. The election of 1977 proved conclusively that Indian voters were not patsies. The Congress had ruled India since independence. No other party had power in villages all across India. The Congress had most of the money and most of the traditional bosses on its side. But Indian voters appeared in great numbers to throw the sainted Congress out of office and try someone new. When the new party proved unsatisfactory, it went the same way. And Rajiv knows only too well that what happened to his mother can happen to him. The democratic impulse, once raised, is too powerful to control with empty promises.

6

Development: Farm and Factory

The poor nations and the well-to-do countries generally face two entirely different sets of problems. The poor nations are usually referred to as "developing" countries because they are still in the process of developing their basic institutions—health care systems, schools, essential industries, and utilities. In the industrialized countries of Europe and North America most of these institutions have already been established, for better or worse, so that the economy in such countries is often thought of as a highly complex machine. You can tinker with it—pump in more or less money, raise or lower taxes—but actually changing the way it works seems almost unthinkable. Most people in these industrialized countries, be they communists or capitalists, have achieved something close to a middle-class life-style and thus have some reason to think that the machine has functioned decently, if not ideally, for them.

In India the vast majority of people are poor, and many are

desperately poor; a small number are quite rich, but so few are they that even if you distributed all their wealth evenly in the country the poor would be not much better off than before. Thus India cannot merely "keep people satisfied"; it has to change their basic status, to free them from poverty and illiteracy and disease and despair. How to face this daunting task? Since independence the country has been asking itself the most fundamental questions: Who will own the wealth? Who will make the most important economic decisions? How much industry do we need and what kind? Should there be big or small farms? In no case has India been satisfied with only one answer to these questions. Beset by the same contradictory influences that we have seen running throughout Indian life, national development has followed a winding path and has produced an economy which, be it good or bad, resembles almost no other economy in the world. We will look first at these contradictory influences and then at the system they have created and are creating.

I The Development of a Poor Nation

Gandhi and Nehru, united in their goal of liberating India from foreign tyranny, parted ways when India became theirs to direct. Each had a complete, consistent vision of a free and modern India, but the two images had little in common. Nehru's was a vision of glory: to the moral greatness of a poor nation taking the risk of democracy he would add the material splendor of modern factories, famous scientific institutions, and noble cities, all run by a vast and efficient bureaucracy. Nehru wished India to be "better" than other countries in that it would not wage war unless provoked and would not deprive citizens of their liberties; at the same time he sought to emulate other nations that were swiftly moving away from the old world of the peasant and countryside and toward the new world of the city and the factory and the modern attitudes that went with that move. Explaining his preference for up-to-date technology and modern industry, Nehru wrote, "In India especially, where we have been wedded far too long to past forms and modes of thought and action, new experiences, new processes, leading to new ideas and new horizons, are necessary."

When Nehru looked for an example of a successful country he often pointed to the Soviet Union or China. Both had begun like India, as vast, unwieldy nations mired in poverty. Through their communist revolutions, Nehru felt, they had discovered a means of accelerating the slow pace of economic change and had brought about a modern, industrious frame of mind in a traditional people. Russia, Nehru wrote admiringly, had undertaken an "amazing and prodigious effort to create a new world out of the dregs of the old." But Nehru saw clearly enough that both countries had crushed the flower of liberty. Nehru wished to borrow from the Russians and Chinese their ability to organize great projects and motivate people to join them, without resorting to their use of brutal police power.

Gandhi's vision could best be described as one of justice, or righteousness, rather than glory. "For me," he said, "there is no distinction between politics and religion." Equally concerned as Nehru with the problem of motivating a sluggish, timid people, Gandhi would have had them look backward for inspiration to their own ancient ideals, rather than forward to an image of wealth and efficiency and material progress. Thus Gandhi was horrified not so much by poverty—he had chosen poverty for himself—as by the gap between the rich and the poor, the denial of equality. The great projects and shining factories with which Nehru and the other westernized leaders were preoccupied left Gandhi cold. "I consider it a sin and injustice," he said, "to use machinery for the purpose of concentration of power and riches in the hands of the few. Today the machine is used in that way."

Gandhi thought in terms of local, rather than national, development, for it was in the villages that the simple lifestyle and traditional values he held dear had been preserved. Gandhi took up spinning cotton on a spinning wheel and urged others to do likewise, not only to make India independent of foreign textile manufacturers but to provide an instance of the kind of economy that India might have— one in which self-sufficient individuals make a livelihood by practicing traditional crafts, thus making machinery unnecessary. Gandhi urged all Congress workers to involve themselves in the so-called Constructive Program of village uplift: digging wells, teaching reading, providing basic medical or agricultural services. Gandhi felt that these programs should be undertaken by individuals on a voluntary basis, not by a government capable of marshaling vast squads of people and resources. The village was to be the material and spiritual center of Gandhi's India, a village characterized by equality, integrity, and stability. The goal of *swaraj,* or self-rule, Gandhi would stress, was *ram raj,* the holy kingdom. Gandhi's India would have been practical, and disciplined, but it would have borne more resemblance to the mythical or idealized communities of the world's holy books than to any nation in the modern world.

These were clashing views. At the moment of independence Gandhi dropped away from the new government like a Moses barred from the Promised Land. He returned to his work in the countryside, aware that the nation had passed into the hands of a class of people he could not expect to control. And three years later, in 1950, he was felled by an assassin's bullet. Nehru's influence waxed as Gandhi's waned, and modern India began to take on its Nehruesque

shape in the early 1950s. Probably the most important event
in this process was the creation of the Planning Commission
in 1950. The whole idea of a planned economy, with its
ministries and files and projects and systems and, above all,
its control violated Gandhi's hopes for an economy based on
simple transactions between individuals or small groups.
The development of the Planning Commission reflected instead the faith that Nehru and most other national leaders
felt in the Soviet Union, whose entire economy was directed
by a series of committees in Moscow. The government
adopted the Russian system of composing five-year plans,
now popular in much of the developing world.

The substance of the first five-year plan and of the other
two plans developed in Nehru's time accelerated the eclipse
of the Gandhian idea of development. Gandhi wished to
emphasize agricultural and village development, though he
would have accomplished such development more through
individual effort than through a government raising and distributing money. The first plan devoted only 15 percent of
the five-year outlay to agriculture and community development, a figure that shrank to 12 percent in the next
plan. Meanwhile, the figure devoted to medium and large
industries and mining rose from 6 percent to 14 percent,
then to 21 percent in the third plan in 1962. India had taken
the industrial machine route, which Gandhi deplored but
toward which the entire world seemed to be gravitating.

During these years a new debate sprang up, one to which
Gandhi seemed almost irrelevant. On one side stood the
socialists, led by Nehru and attracted to the Soviet, and
increasingly the Chinese, economic systems, and on the
other the capitalists, led by businessmen and many older
politicians, who looked toward the United States as an example of development. Nehru more or less won this battle, too.
By 1954 he had begun speaking of the need for a "socialistic

pattern of development," and he succeeded in arguing that the government should occupy the "commanding heights" of the economy—transportation, communication, and most of the basic industries. We will go into this debate at length later on.

It would be wrong to think that Nehru's modern idea of development simply trounced Gandhi's traditional concept, just as it would be mistaken to think that the Congress successfully neutralized all opposition, or, for that matter, that Hinduism triumphed over Islam. Indian history—above all, its modern history—can be understood only as a series of muffled clashes, uncomfortable alliances, wobbly compromises, neglected contradictions—the process, in short, of highly unlike people learning to live with one another in a time of rapid change.

Gandhi's disciples have never ceased to spread the gospel of voluntarism, small-scale development, and village self-rule. Nor were Nehru and other leaders hostile to much of Gandhi's program. The eradication of untouchability, which Gandhi held at the very center of his principles, has always been a basic concern of the government. Nehru, much of whose tutoring about village India came from Gandhi, believed with Gandhi that equality was the most important principle in village-level development and concerned himself passionately with breaking the stranglehold of wealthy landowners. India's vast system of "cottage industries"— small, state-supported businesses performing largely traditional crafts—certainly owes its birth to Gandhi. And Gandhi's emphasis on voluntary work has never left India and continues to provide an important first step for young men considering careers in politics. Throughout the 1950s Vinoba Bhave, a revered Gandhian, walked from village to village across northern India, asking large landowners to give some of their land to the community. From time to time Bhave announced impressive gifts of land, but later inspection proved that most of the acreage was unfarmable and was, in any case, sold rather than given and then bought back by the same landlords at reduced prices. Gandhi probably would have known better than to place so much faith in human nature, but Bhave's failure did seem to confirm that the one thing that politics can least change is people.

II Farming

Since the great majority of Indians are farmers, our judgment of the problems and successes of the Indian economy must begin with an understanding of agriculture. The single most important distinction among Indian farmers divides those who own enough land to support themselves from those who do not. The size of the average landholding in India has been shrinking steadily as the population has grown, so that by now only half of the farmers have plots big enough to provide a livelihood. A farmer with less than two and a half acres usually has trouble supporting himself and his family and will probably become a sharecropper. In many states sharecropping is illegal, but it continues nevertheless. As many as one-third of the 500 million Indians who make their living from agriculture have no land at all, and this figure, too, has been rising steadily. This great mass of people, most of them low-caste, must eke out a precarious existence wholly dependent on the farmers who employ them on their land. Their average wage amounts to slightly under a dollar a day in most parts of India, and work generally cannot be found on more than half the days in the year. A dollar, of course, buys far more in India than in America: two pounds each of rice, onions, and lentils, a handful of chili peppers, and perhaps a pint of milk. But after two meager meals a day a family has next to nothing left for any kind of expenditure at all, and a sudden change of fortune—illness or crop failure—may cut them down to one meal, or none at all.

The principal problem faced by most self-sufficient farmers is how to increase the number and quality of their crops. Since rain falls only three months out of the year in almost all of India, farmers do not have the water to grow more than one crop each year without irrigation, and barely one-third of Indian farmland is irrigated. Much of the water for irrigation comes from reservoirs, some of them built centuries ago, that feed a network of hand-dug trenches running from one tiny plot to another. Reservoir water generally dries up by November or December but still lasts long enough to permit a second crop. Another popular form of irrigation is the tube well, which is made by sinking a tube into the earth until it strikes an underground source of water. Only a well-to-do farmer can afford to dig one himself, but the government also supplies them.

But irrigation is only one link in a long and precarious chain on which the Indian farmers depend. A tube well, for example, does a farmer no good without the electricity or diesel fuel to run it. One of India's most heartbreaking and complex problems has been the shortage of electricity, with power plants producing at only 40 percent of their capacity. Blackouts are common, factories frequently shut down, and some villages receive power no more than three or four hours a day, sometimes in the middle of the night. And the price of diesel fuel, like that of all oil products, has skyrocketed, so that it is often unavailable or unaffordable. Thus farmers are not only ill-equipped but also unable to use their equipment fully.

Since chemical, or nitrogen-based, fertilizers, work only in combination with a great deal of water, a farmer without adequate irrigation is forced to use manure instead, a tradi-

The traditional rice harvest, in Tamil Nadu (Photo courtesy of Air India)

tional but vastly inferior fertilizer. And good fertilizers, like electricity, are simply not available in sufficient quantity. The use of chemical fertilizers has revolutionized India's crop output, especially in wheat, but the daring farmer who switches from manure often finds that the shelves of his local cooperative are bare. And without fertilizer, the farmer can't use many of the new high-yielding strains of rice and wheat developed during the "Green Revolution" of the last fifteen years. Farmers who have changed to these varieties have as much as doubled their production, but disaster results if the farmer buys the new seed and cannot find or afford the fertilizer they require.

And for any of these investments the farmer needs credit, especially the small farmer who makes almost no profit at all.

120

Every village has a moneylender, but with interest at 30 percent a year or more, most villagers will resort to him only in times of emergency. In an effort to make investments easier for the small farmer the government has sent branches of its state-owned banks into the countryside and established a system of rural cooperatives that offer credit. Yet the banks cover only a fraction of the countryside, and the cooperatives generally fall into the hands of the big landlords and merchants, who deny loans to the needy and provide them to the well-heeled, who are then permitted to dally about repayment.

When the chain that stretches from credit to seed packets functions well, Indian farmers sometimes perform great feats of productivity. Farmers in Punjab, for example, pro-

Modern farming in Punjab (Photo courtesy of the Indian Embassy to the United States)

duce twice as much wheat and rice per acre as farmers elsewhere in India; they produce more wheat per acre—more than a ton—than Americans with their fantastic machinery and usually dependable rainfall. The Green Revolution ushered in with the new high-yielding seeds was introduced in Punjab and transformed the state almost overnight. Crop yield doubled in less than a decade; tractors and tube wells appeared everywhere; the demand for credit grew insatiably. An entirely new class of wealthy, modern, businesslike farmers grew up in the state, especially around the agricultural university in Ludhiana. Although there can be no doubt that the smallest farmers and the landless benefited relatively little from these events, the average Punjabi is better fed, better educated, better housed, and more long-lived than other Indians.

Many people believe that Punjab provides a source of hope for India's future, but the state stands as something of a special example. Nowhere in India is water quite so plentiful or land so fairly distributed. And the Sikhs who make up much of Punjab's population are, as they are fond of pointing out, far more aggressive and daring than the average Indian farmer.

Another special example is Bihar, whose dire poverty indicates the obstacles that India's poorest peasants must face. In contrast to Punjab's fairly equal distribution of land, Bihar is divided among an old, aristocratic class of landlords, called *zamindars*; a huge, growing class of tenant farmers and landless peasants; and the recently created, aggressive group of farmers with middle-sized holdings known as Jats. Zamindars may own anywhere from 50 to 10,000 acres, despite laws that prohibit the ownership of more than 18 acres per household. The zamindars have been less concerned with improving their land than with retaining power over the hundreds of peasants who labor for them. Northern Bihar, for example, is divided by rivers, but irrigation systems are few. Neither high-yielding seeds nor fertilizers sell well. And this neglect of modern farming has led to a generally poor quality of life: illiteracy is common, health care is poor, electrified villages are rare.

Most Biharis who earn their living from the soil cannot even begin to think about fancy seeds and fertilizer. They have neither the land to make them useful nor the money to afford them. Improvements in the land they farm for someone else would raise their own standard of living slightly but would not free them from dependence. Their hard work gets them nowhere, and they can find little prospect for change. For them, and for the almost two-thirds of Indian farm workers who own either no land or too little to be self-sufficient, another answer must be found. They must either be given some of the land that now belongs to the wealthier farmers or they must be allowed to find additional or altogether different work. And here the governments of free India have faced some of their most troubling dilemmas.

III Land Reform and Village Power

Nearly everyone in India is in favor of land reform. Clearly the presence of a handful of people who own hundreds or thousands of acres in the midst of a crowd of marginal farmers and landless peasants offends the Directive Principles of State Policy. Five-year plans since 1952 have reiterated the necessity of bold land reform, and every state in the nation was compelled, starting in the late 1950s, to pass laws requiring the distribution of "excess" lands. But in thirty years barely more than one million acres have changed hands, while the various state land reform laws would make at least 22 million acres available.

Land reform's sluggish progress provides perhaps the best example of the problems that India has had with its federal system and helps explain how true democracy sometimes hinders development in a poor nation. Nehru championed land reform from the start, believing, with every justification, that farmers would work harder for themselves than for others. But the states thwarted him at every corner. Mrs. Gandhi made land reform a crucial part of her ten-point program and, later, her twenty-point program. By this time state governments were no longer actively opposing such steps; they were simply refusing, by and large, to do anything about them.

Why have the states proved so reluctant to enforce land reform laws? Largely because big landlords, whose land would be confiscated, have been heavily represented in the state assemblies. And the closer one gets to the village, the greater the landlord's power becomes. If a landlord takes into his head to bribe or bully a local official into falsifying land records, he may very well get away with it. A favorite ploy is to put excess land in the name of a relative, a servant, or even a pet; and the government clerk turns a blind eye.

What can the government in Delhi do under these circumstances? Perhaps it could put more pressure on state leaders to bring about authentic land reform. But India's federal system reserves power over agricultural issues for the states, and the central government can do little more than watch. A democracy—and especially a federal democracy—often has trouble making reform move swiftly, because power is distributed broadly; one group can obstruct the will of another, especially when the obstructors are powerful.

Even the most effective land reform program, however, would still leave a great many farmers with tiny plots: there simply isn't enough land to go around. These people must be given some other work that does not force them to leave their villages.

Farm life itself offers a wide variety of jobs beyond the fields: raising pigs and poultry, stocking fish ponds, dairy farming, vegetable gardening. Wth such jobs the peasant remains in the village, earns money, and provides a useful service. Even the smallest farmer, for example, usually has a cow or a buffalo for farming, but he could also be using them for milk. Before independence farmers in Gujarat used to sell small amounts of milk to traders who kept prices low, keeping much of the profit for themselves. After independence a cooperative was formed. It began offering cattle owners veterinary services, free pickup, processing, marketing, and, above all, high prices, in exchange for joining. Peasants saw a good thing and started to join in large numbers. Today the Anand cooperative, as it is called, has over a quarter-million members and markets more than $100 million worth of dairy products annually—and this in only one district in one state. Small farmers, using only what they already have—a cow or a buffalo—have found themselves earning half again their daily wage, or more. Tenants and landless laborers feel freed from their employer, the landlord, since they now enjoy another source of income. The Indian government now backs the Anand cooperative enthusiastically and has begun to believe that similar projects could succeed in putting money in the peasant's pocket.

We have spoken of many of the problems the Indian peasants face and of the government's effort to solve them, but what all these attempts boil down to is the goal of changing the ancient power structure of the village. The peasants can vote and voice their opinions, but village life, as we have been pointing out, is hardly democratic: a handful of people rule the destiny of the rest, and Untouchables continue to be practically excluded from society.

Nehru and Gandhi were in perfect agreement on the need to liberate the peasants from their dependence on the powerful; Nehru cherished this goal above almost any other, resisting programs that might increase village prosperity but also increase the power of the rich over the poor. He sought to use India's democracy to give the majority of villagers— that is, the poor ones—the opportunity to control the money and the goods that were coming to them through the country's development program. Thus he worked to give more power to the panchayats and to set up a system of cooperatives through which farmers could purchase most of their supplies.

Cooperatives, which are organizations owned by all their members, play a crucial role in Indian life. We have already mentioned the Anand dairy cooperative; one of the crucial features of the Anand system is that the farmers vote on all the group's important decisions and decide themselves what to do with the village's profits. It is hard to imagine how important this can be to a person accustomed to exercising no authority at all. Most villagers also belong to cooperatives that sell fertilizer, seed, even tractors, and that offer loans at low rates. The idea behind these cooperatives, first championed by Gandhi and established in the 1950s, was that they would be directed by poor peasants themselves for their own betterment.

But cooperatives, like panchayats, rarely fall under the control of the weak members of the village. We mentioned before that credit cooperatives routinely deny peasants loans; the reason for this is that the same tiny group that controls most of the village's wealth and runs the panchayat also sits on the board of the cooperative.

Neither cooperatives nor panchayats have really fulfilled their original purpose of wresting power away from the few and giving it to the many. If economic development is to be judged a failure in India—and that would be unfairly harsh—the principal reason would be the government's inability to lift the poor peasant from generations of dependence.

But the old system of obligation and obedience has begun to dissolve under the pressure of economic change, advances in communication and transportation, and the fight for political power in the panchayats and cooperatives. The poor are demanding their rights after having submitted to their plight for centuries. Landless laborers have begun to insist that they be paid the minimum wage, which states guarantee by law, or that they be permitted to use some of the common land held by the government. Landlords, in turn, have recognized that this new aggressiveness threatens their own power and have struck back. Though Indians are usually thought of as tranquil, peaceable people, the countryside has been wracked by savage battles between low-caste laborers and high-caste landowners, as the government stands by helplessly.

Much of the blood has been shed in Bihar or in the eastern half of its neighbor, Uttar Pradesh, where conditions are also backward. A group of low-caste laborers might occupy a parcel of common land that a local landlord has illegally claimed as his own. Then the grim drama unfolds. The infuriated landlord, who has never before been defied by a member of a low caste, decides to intimidate the laborers to make sure this will never happen again. He goes into town and hires a gang of thugs, a private army equipped with clubs, knives, and, sometimes, guns. The marauders arrive in the village with torches blazing and head for the low-caste encampment. There they destroy everything in sight—huts, shops, cattle sheds, bicycles, food. Not infrequently they burn down huts with peasants still cowering inside them. Women are raped, men and children severely beaten, sometimes horribly murdered. And where are the police? Often enough the police know about the attack, but out of either fear for their safety or sympathy with the landlord they are careful to arrive on the scene as slowly as possible. It is hard to see what will put an end to this violence.

Governments have done little to relieve the frustrations of the poor, though their promises sound bold, and the nation's leaders can do little about the insecurity of landlords without putting a stop to all reform. But the violence has been concentrated in the areas that most resist change. The fissures that divide India are growing deeper and deeper, making violence almost unavoidable, but where the needs of the poor are neglected, such bloodshed is certain to occur.

IV *Industrial Development versus Traditional Economy*

Indians are fond of referring to their country as "the world's tenth greatest industrial power," though the ranking changes depending on what standards are used. The middle-aged recall that at the time of independence almost everything from toothpaste to paper to automobiles had to be imported. Today India stands almost alone among developing nations in supplying all the needs of its consumers from its own factories. India has also become a major exporting nation, sending abroad goods worth more than $7 billion. Like many poor nations, India exports mostly raw materials, like nuts or tobacco or fibers, and the products of cheap labor, such as clothing or footwear. But India has also become a major exporter of iron and steel products, placing it alongside other such new industrial powers as South Korea and Brazil.

India exports not only merchandise but also talent. Every year thousands of engineers leave from Bombay for the Middle East and Africa. Indians run the entire railway system of Nigeria and direct the huge construction sites in the Persian Gulf. Throughout the developing world Indians are looked upon as the most skilled professionals and technicians available, save those from the industrial countries. Only the United States and the Soviet Union have as large a body of scientists as this new nation. The quality of many of India's engineering institutes, as well as its graduate schools in business and medicine, matches, and possibly surpasses, that of any other poor nation.

Thirty years of industrial and professional development have shocked India out of its old slumber and brought about a great change in values, but the change has not proved a strong enough lever to wrench the country from poverty.

For this reason India's industrial development has come under fire from all sides. Gandhians would just as soon tear down many of the huge factories and glittering computers and fancy hotels and do away with the whole westernized middle class that operates this new economy. Businessmen point to the country's low rates of growth—a steady 3 percent—and accuse the government of stifling free enterprise. Workers feel underpaid and neglected and help slow the economy by going on strike or working at half speed to protest their conditions.

The clash between the philosophies of Gandhi and Nehru has been far clearer in debate over industry and business than in discussions of rural development. Gandhi feared that major industrial development would corrupt his people; Nehru believed that its absence would condemn them to poverty and backwardness. Gandhi favored a small government—or, ideally, no government at all—while Nehru believed in the need for a dominating government, raising and spending large amounts of money. At first Nehru moved cautiously, approving a modest five-year plan with sizable rural investments. But as the economy poked along in the early 1950s, Nehru and his associates became convinced that economic growth ought to proceed full throttle, fueled by government spending. The second plan foresaw the government raising and distributing twice as much money as it had under the first plan, with industrial development receiving five times the total amount of aid devoted to it five years earlier. From this time the government tried to strain its limits as much as possible, raising money through increased taxation and borrowing, funneling large amounts into industry and related fields like power and transportation, and setting high goals for growth. Although the goals were never reached—the economy grew at its plodding 3 percent pace while other nations shot forward two or three times as quickly—the early planners of India's economy managed to create the modern industry, the large pool of skilled professionals, and the vast railway network that the country now enjoys.

But the debate between the village and the factory has not subsided. Proponents of industry point out that villagers, too, depend on factories—for cement to build roads connecting village and town, for paper used in the local school, for power to run tube wells. More important, they argue, industrial development serves as an engine for growth, since profits produce money that people can invest and spend, thus helping other business grow. They argue further that the government can tax, thus permitting it to spend more money on its own programs. Gandhians characteristically object to this line of thought on the moral ground that the wealth created by big business is evil—an argument against capitalism—and that traditional Indian values cannot survive the shift to an industrial society. Economists, however, assert that the money and the goods produced by industry do not work their way down to the village level. The only way to bring prosperity to the village, they believe, is for the government to spend its money there, on irrigation, power, employment, social services and the like.

The brief reign of the Janata government provided India with an experiment in rural development. Many of the Congress's stalwart Gandhians, unhappy with Mrs. Gandhi, joined the new party and helped shape its economic policies. Charan Singh, the finance minister and later prime minister, had churned out a towering pile of pamphlets denouncing industrial development, showing the way to a policy of growth based on the farmer, and advocating, if at all possible, the toppling of skyscrapers and the bulldozing of factories.

In collaboration with less passionate economists, Singh

produced a new five-year plan that shifted government expenditure from industry to the villages. Though the Janata later discredited itself through political wrangling, the government oversaw a small revolution in rural employment programs, electrification, and irrigation (skyscrapers and hotels remained intact). The Janata experiment was to involve more than a mere change in budget. Party manifestos advocated a broad Gandhian program of restoring strength to the villages and reversing the trend toward a large, domineering central government in favor of granting more power to state and local governments. Mrs. Gandhi's victory, however, wiped out these budding plans. But many of the Janata's rural programs have been kept intact, reflecting a new belief among economists that the government should, in fact, spend more money in the villages.

Another topic of contention between Gandhians and their opponents is whether industry should consist primarily of huge factories with the most modern technology, like those in the major economic powers, or of many smaller factories, in the traditional fashion. Gandhi felt a deep antipathy toward the big textile mills, though he often sought help from their owners in his battle against the British. Gandhi objected, first, to the dehumanizing influence of the "big machine" and of the cities in which such factories were normally located. His second objection was to the destruction of traditional weaving crafts that cheap mill-made cloth brought about. And, third, he objected to the modern factory's need for large amounts of money but small amounts of labor; such factories, he believed, exacerbated India's employment problem. The argument has not abated but has come to revolve more and more around the third point.

Gandhi's influence led the new government to protect the small-scale and "tiny" manufacturers from the large-scale industries. Over 500 products cannot by law be made by industries worth over $100,000, thus allowing small business to flourish without competition from giant factories. The government prohibits large factories from producing more than a specific quantity of certain other goods, leaving aside a set amount for small-scale enterprises. Mills have been especially restricted in this way, in order to leave room for the government-funded *khadi,* or homespun, program. Certain kinds of clothing can be made only on hand looms or small power looms.

The government wouldn't have to spend anything at all, nor would it have to erect any special barriers, if people wanted to buy what the small- and tiny-scale industries produced at the price for which they could produce them. But history proves that machines, because they work more cheaply and efficiently, tend to replace people.

Clothing made in a mill costs a good deal less than clothing turned out on a loom and is likely to be better, if plainer. This poses a great dilemma to India's economic planners. On the one hand, machines cost less than people and do better work, but, at least in the short run, they increase unemployment. To disregard the machines, on the other hand, is to waste precious money.

By now India simply cannot do without the giant, efficient factory; its huge, multibillion-dollar economy cannot be fed from the thousand tiny streams of cottage industries. But the terrible danger of the "big machine," especially in a poor nation largely ignorant of the hazards of industry, was proven with terrible force in December 1984. Shortly after midnight one cool winter's night a deadly gas escaped from a tank at the Union Carbide plant in Bhopal, in the central state of Madhya Pradesh. The gas was called methyl isocyanate, a chemical used in making pesticides. Everyone at the factory, and some of the surrounding townspeople, had heard that the compound was dangerous; but no one had any

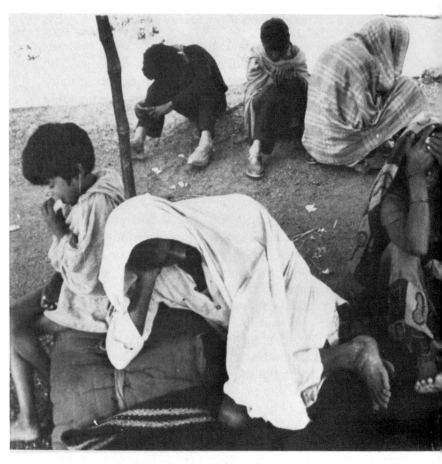

Thousands of people were stricken by poisonous gas that leaked from the Union Carbide pesticide factory in Bhopal, India, in December 1984 (Photo courtesy of AP/Wide World)

idea how lethal it was until that night. Within an hour all 45 tons of the gas had leaked out, and spread across several miles of the city. First the cattle toppled over and died. Then slum-dwellers near the plant began to rub their eyes violently, then to vomit, then to gasp for air, finally to die from an accumulation of fluid in the lungs. Within a few days the hospitals were choked, and the corpses were everywhere. At least 2,500 people died; another 200,000 were hospitalized. It was the worst industrial accident in history.

Later investigation showed that the parent American company had not built in as many safeguards in Bhopal as it had in its factories in the United States. It was equally clear that the local managers had disregarded warnings of safety lapses, and that ill-trained, ill-prepared personnel had been unable to prevent the accident or to deal with it once it started. The Bhopal disaster proved the need for greater vigilance and care in handling deadly substances, but it started no major anti-industry movement. India knows that it wants to be a modern nation; there can be no question of turning back to the spinning wheel.

V *Socialism: The Planned Economy*

The influence of Gandhi has given India a unique set of policies and problems, but from the outset India has faced a dilemma confronted by all Third World nations: whether to construct a socialist or a capitalist economy. Like most of these new countries India has chosen a combination of the two, with the government entirely controlling some industries, partially involved in others, and leaving certain fields wholly to private business. But while much of the Third World, even such communist countries as China, has moved toward a more flexible, more capitalist economy, India has stuck to the highly planned form of socialism it adopted in the 1950s. The trend elsewhere in the world has emboldened India's businessmen and many of its economists to call on the government to release its tight grip on business and investment and to turn over much government-owned industry to private enterprise. Well-educated young Indians increasingly opt for careers in business rather than govern-

ment and regard socialism as an old-fashioned philosophy more suited to the days of independence than to modern times.

Nehru and the generation of intellectuals he led grew up in the aftermath of the Russian revolution and were deeply influenced by the Russian example. Socialism seemed to liberate people from the economic tyranny of the rich just as the independence struggle had liberated them from the tyranny of the colonialists. Freedom and socialism went hand in hand. Nehru was engaged in constant battle with capitalists in the Congress, but in 1954 he announced that India was to be a socialist country. By this statement Nehru meant two

Workers making khadi—cotton woven on hand looms (Photo courtesy of the Indian Embassy to the United States)

things. First, he was making it clear that the government would have a controlling interest in basic industries. Thus the government of India serves as the country's sole producer of coal, oil, and power; it runs the railways and the telephone and telegraph systems; it owns the banks and the life insurance company; it produces much of the steel and cement. These industries and services are so important to the national well-being that Nehru believed private interests should not be permitted to take a large part in directing them.

The second thing that Nehru had in mind was that the government would plan and supervise even those parts of the economy that it did not run. The entire economy—rural and urban, small-scale and large-scale, public and private—would be seen as one vast, interconnected enterprise that only the government could coordinate. No essential decision could be made without its approval. If a business wished to build a new factory or sell a new product, it would need a license from the government; it could not produce more of its product than the government permitted; and it could not own any business abroad, since this might upset the careful balance constructed in the five-year plan (and permit it to hide its profits as well).

India's socialist system has had its ups and downs. Shastri, on the one hand, had little sympathy for the government's large role and was moving in the direction of private enterprise at the time of his death. Mrs. Gandhi, on the other hand, was a more or less instinctive socialist, like her father. She also realized—while her power was still insecure—that she could make herself popular by denouncing capitalists for trying to violate the public interest. Thus, in 1969, she put her ten-point program into effect, nationalizing banks and insurance companies. Two years later she pushed through the Foreign Exchange Restriction Act, preventing foreign companies from owning more than a 40 percent interest in their branches in India. Rajiv Gandhi, though, may prove to be India's first out-and-out capitalist prime minister. Most of his friends are businessmen rather than politicians, and he knows their problems well. Indian socialism may be dismantled during his tenure.

Though businessmen everywhere complain about government regulation, businessmen in India are more hemmed in by restrictions than most. Should they run their factories so efficiently that they produce more than their official quota, they will be penalized. Should they wish to use their profits to expand, they may not be permitted to do so. Every im-

A warp spinning machine in a Bombay cotton mill (Photo courtesy of the Indian Embassy to the United States)

portant decision must be taken up with an increasingly sleepy bureaucracy, where it may disappear in a labyrinth of offices and office holders. Small businessmen—a rapidly growing class who might do much to alleviate urban unemployment—feel especially frustrated, pointing out that the government usually favors a handful of gigantic family-run businesses at the expense of entrepreneurs like themselves. With India continuing to falter in its economic growth, their arguments may be heeded.

Should the government own so much of basic industry? Indian businessmen, like businessmen everywhere, claim that they would run the industries more efficiently than the state does. India's state-run coal mines, for example, suffer from antiquated equipment and frequent work stoppages; the state-run railways that load the coal lack the cars to do the job adequately; the state-owned power stations that burn the coal operate at as little as 40 percent of their capacity. Businessmen and many economists believe that a competitive system might improve on these results. State-run enterprises as a whole usually turn a very small profit, despite huge government outlays. One notable exception is the railways, which carry more passengers over more miles than any other railway system in the world. Despite charging under eight dollars for a twenty-hour trip, the railways usually report a significant profit.

The whole planning system, however, depends on government control of basic industries. The state not only produces the steel, coal, cement, and so forth, but decides what to do with it—when and where to build roads, dams, schools, military equipment, and the like. If power is scarce, as it is sure to remain in the foreseeable future, who is to decide how much should be devoted to factories and how much to villages? The state will decide as long as it controls both the coal and the generators. In the end the dispute over public or private ownership comes down to this question: Who will safeguard the national interest better—the state or private enterprise?

For the several million Indians who actually work in factories, the question of ownership does not make a great deal of difference. Many Indians work in conditions reminiscent of turn-of-the-century industry in England or the United States. Air conditioning is rare in this torrid country; hours are long; the work place is often unclean; protections are few (one can watch a man work steel at a small forge without goggles or mask); and laborers go home to tiny, dark, cramped barracks. But the salary of 50 dollars a month and up puts the worker far ahead of the farmer; in fact, foremen sometimes charge an eager laborer an "entrance fee" of as much as a thousand rupees (80 dollars) for a position in a factory. The conditions, abysmal as they are, could not be improved much without making most businesses unprofitable. For this reason, perhaps, industrial violence has not been as great in India as in many other countries.

But agitation has been increasing in recent years. Mrs. Gandhi crushed a nationwide railway strike in 1974 by summarily clapping in jail, first, 600 leaders and, then, 20,000 workers. The mine workers, members of a union controlled by the CPI—each of the major Indian unions is affiliated with a political party—have been paralyzing or slowing work at coal mines in Bihar and West Bengal for a number of years, with no end in sight. A bloody strike closed down the massive Tata Steel Works in Jamshedpur, Uttar Pradesh, in 1979. The class violence that has begun to sweep the countryside started in a smaller way in the cities and work places. Violence may be thought of as one of the inevitable growing pains of a poor nation in the modern world, where changes that once took centuries are compressed into decades. At the same time violence must be understood as a challenge to that society—a challenge to satisfy the needy so far as is possible, to restrain the powerful, and to promote a sense of fairness that binds all together.

7
India and the World

When India shocked the world by detonating an atomic bomb in the desert of Gujarat on May 19, 1974, it officially laid to rest the idealistic, open-handed foreign policy that had dominated its first fifteen years as an independent nation. India joined the modern world of threat and warfare. Only thirteen years earlier Nehru responded to a question about defense spending by saying, "Today there is a conflict in the world between two things, the atom bomb, and what it represents, and the spirit of humanity." India, he said, "will always lay stress on the spirit of humanity." At that time free India's soldiers had never clashed with a foreign army. But over the next decade India suffered, or provoked, three invasions, and Nehru's sentiments began to seem like empty piety. Though India's borders have remained inviolate since 1971, the country's foreign policy is based on securing its borders and ensuring its military strength, where once it had revolved, somewhat improbably, around the promotion of harmony among developing nations. But one of the standards of Nehru's day has stood, if shakily, before the winds of war: the determination to steer clear of excessive dependence on either the United States or the Soviet Union.

I Nehru: The Philosopher of Nonalignment

Nehru was driven by a powerful missionary spirit, a spirit he felt moving his nation as well as himself. India's persistent independence struggle and its dedication to democratic principles had already made it a shining example to the world. Now, Nehru believed, his nation must continue to prove its special destiny by conducting itself before the world with the same high-mindedness. As India had pursued its own liberation nonviolently, so it could work to reduce bloodshed by teaching, Nehru said, "that physical force need not necessarily be the arbiter of man's destiny"— a powerful proof of Gandhi's influence on Nehru. Toward this end Nehru made himself an ardent spokesman for peace in international councils and sought to place India between combatants, rather than on either side. In 1956 India helped negotiate an end to the Suez crisis involving Egypt and England, and three years earlier it had directed the prisoner exchange between the United States and North Korea at the end of the Korean War.

Nehru wished to make India's relations with China a model of international cooperation. Nehru felt a deep sense of kinship with the Chinese, who had also thrown off the yoke of tyranny, and he admired what he saw as their great economic progress. The two nations were neighbors and would show the world that neighbors could live in peace. In 1951 Nehru visited China and concluded an agreement, known as the Panch Sheel, or Five Principles, pledging the two nations to respect each other's borders and conduct

themselves peaceably. Indian economic planners and
scholars visited China frequently, Sino-Indian Friendship
Societies sprouted, and visiting Chinese dignitaries were
greeted with the cry, *Hindi Chini bhai bhai*—"Friendship
between Indian and Chinese people." Nehru wished to extend the Panch Sheel to other nations, but he was unable to
conclude any equally grandiose agreements.

It was just as well that Nehru was unable to pursue Panch
Sheel any further, because the Chinese proved how dedicated they were to fine promises by, first, violating India's
borders and then, in 1962, invading India itself. The Chinese had begun building the Aksai Chin road through territory that both countries claimed along the northeast frontier.
Nehru knew about the construction of the road as early as
1957 but refused to regard it as a belligerent act and con-
cealed it from the public for two years. But the Chinese
expanded their claims to include over 15,000 square miles of
territory along the entire northern border. Skirmishes broke
out between the two sides, culminating in a Chinese invasion from the northeast. Grossly unprepared and under-
manned Indian troops were routed. The Chinese advanced
at will and then, having proved their point, withdrew to the
position they had held in 1959. India's humiliation, still re-
membered vividly today, fell upon the defense minister,
Krishna Menon, and on Nehru himself. The policy of peaceful coexistence was discredited, the Chinese stood revealed
to many Indians as cynics, and Nehru's experiment in international living drew to a close.

A more enduring legacy, however, was Nehru's policy of
nonalignment. In the aftermath of World War II many of the
new nations believed that an exclusive alliance with either
the United States or the Soviet Union would jeopardize
their precious independence and restore them to a more
subtle form of their old colonial status. Leaders like Tito of

Yugoslavia, Nasser of Egypt, and Sukarno of Indonesia decided that they would have to chart a third course—hence the name Third World—in order to weather the growing storm between the communist and capitalist sides without being swallowed by either. Nehru soon emerged as the most ardent advocate of this independent course, outlining the idea of a third force at the historic Bandung conference of nonaligned nations in 1956.

Nonalignment has been frequently misunderstood as a political version of Hindu nonattachment. Nehru had nothing of the sort in mind. As he put it, "We do not wish to be isolated. We wish to have the closest contacts, because we do from the beginning firmly believe in the world coming closer together and ultimately realizing the ideal of what is now being called One World." Nonalignment did not mean neutrality, as it has, for example, in Switzerland. In Nehru's mind it was connected to such concepts as nonviolence, for only by not taking sides against one another could the nations of the world cease the global civil war that Nehru saw developing around him. India's intervention between the Americans and the North Koreans thus stands as an ideal act of nonalignment.

The principal difficulty with nonalignment was, and is, dealing with the United States and the Soviet Union. Nehru felt as deeply drawn to the democratic ideals of the United States as he did to the economic and social revolution achieved by the Soviets. But from the outset Russia gave encouragement and aid to budding national liberation movements—in Vietnam, for example—while the United States almost invariably propped up unpopular conservative leaders. Nehru, with his highly moral view of foreign policy, felt far more sympathetic toward the emerging Russian role in the world. When the United States signed up Pakistan for its new Asian defense alliance, CENTO, in 1954, Nehru moved closer to the Soviets, concluding his first major trade agreement with them the following year.

But Nehru had no intention of enlisting in the Soviet camp, and in 1956 he visited the United States, offering assurances of his nonaligned status. The next year the Americans expanded their aid program in India from $93 million to $365 million. Although the Russians have been instrumental in building up such crucial industries as steel, India has always depended heavily on aid programs from the United States, which have totaled over $7 billion since independence. Some 40 percent of this figure has come in the form of food, which has often tided India over during crisis periods. These outlays were especially important during Nehru's time, so the Indian leader often found himself smoothing ruffled American feathers after publicly criticizing American foreign policy or voting against it in the United Nations.

The crucial events in India's relations with both the United States and the Soviet Union have been the two wars with Pakistan, in 1965 and 1971, especially the latter. A Pakistani resolution in the U.N. Security Council to condemn India for refusing to let Kashmir freely choose to belong either to India or Pakistan was vetoed by the Soviet Union, though supported by the United States. After the war that ensued in 1965, the Soviets quickly stepped in to offer themselves as peacemakers, thus drawing closer to both sides.

The United States had stopped sending arms to Pakistan after the war, but it resumed in 1969, wishing to use the country as a bulwark against the Soviets. Once again India turned toward the Soviet Union, as it had in 1955. Now the Russians supplied whatever military equipment the Indians felt they needed for a possible new attack by Pakistan. When the second war came, in 1971, word leaked out from Washington to the effect that the Nixon administration favored the Pakistanis. When Secretary of State Henry Kissinger stopped over in Delhi on his way to China, during the first days of the war, he admitted that the United States would not defend India in case of a second Chinese invasion. Kissinger's subsequent talks with Chinese leader Mao Zedong and China's new alliance with Pakistan convinced Indian policy makers that the United States was trying to form a three-way agreement against the Soviet Union and India. The passage of fifteen peaceful years has barely dimmed these feelings, and Indians frequently recall that the Pakistanis used American weapons against them in 1965 and 1971.

II Nonalignment without Nehru

As the United States became convinced, in the 1970s, that Indian sympathies lay on the Soviet side, efforts to win India slowed considerably, until Indo-American relations became a matter of small concern. Mrs. Gandhi did, in fact, bitterly criticize the United States for its conduct in Vietnam and elsewhere, and she permitted pro-Soviet advisers to gain great influence in her cabinet and external affairs ministry. At the same time Mrs. Gandhi, like her father, made the obligatory pilgrimage to the United States to ensure the supply of aid and food in the late sixties and, unlike her father, felt no strong sense of spiritual bond for the Soviet system.

As for Rajiv Gandhi, it's altogether possible that, at the time of his sudden elevation to the prime ministership, he had no firm convictions about nonalignment, or foreign policy in general. He seems to share the basic feeling of most middle-class young Indians, that American capitalism is infinitely preferable to Soviet communism, and that the

United States is, in general, a far more attractive country than the Soviet Union or any of its allies. American diplomats are hoping that he will "tilt" toward the United States; but he will probably not tilt very far. Nonalignment seems to be as firmly enshrined in India's foreign policy as secularism is in its constitution.

Nonalignment under Mrs. Gandhi became a strategy for self-defense, a way of playing off one power against another to make India's military situation as secure as possible; Nehru's concern for solidarity with other Third World nations lost much of its importance, while his moral passion, linking nonalignment to world peace, has come to seem outdated. India's military record has not been bad—one loss, one draw, and one resounding victory—but Indians now feel far more insecure than they did in Nehru's day, and they consider aggressiveness a safer defense than idealism.

III Relations with Pakistan

Pakistan remains India's principal antagonist, as it has been since partition. The principal bone of contention between them has been Kashmir, a predominantly Muslim state that many Pakistanis believe would elect to leave India for Pakistan if given the choice. Pakistan always encouraged Kashmiri nationalism, and in 1965 a group of Pakistanis were permitted to cross into Kashmir to help "liberate" part of the territory. The battle that ensued soon drew in the armies of both nations in a swampy area known as the Rann of Kutch. The battle proved inconclusive—the Indians still claim that they won—and was finally stopped when other nations cut off the supply of arms to both sides. But Indians now felt that their worst fears about Pakistani intentions had been borne out; the country began preparing for a second war.

By the time the second one erupted, in 1971, the Indians

had greatly modernized and expanded their army and air force. A civil war had broken out between East and West Pakistan, and ten million East Pakistani refugees streamed into neighboring West Bengal to escape the carnage. India began providing secret aid and equipment to the East Pakistani rebels in hope that their victory would not only divide Pakistan into two weaker nations but also bring about a speedy return of the refugees. The West Pakistanis decided to remove India from the picture by launching an air attack on northeastern India, including Calcutta. This time the Indian military was prepared; in two weeks it swept through East Bengal, smashing the Pakistani army and forcing an unconditional surrender. Mrs. Gandhi dictated the terms of the peace and reached the zenith of her popularity.

Over a decade has passed since the Pakistani invasion and still another decade since the Chinese war, but India continues to patrol its borders with a wary eye. The Chinese have shown no sign of hostility since the war, and the Pakistanis, not much less hostile than usual—the holocaust of Partition cannot be forgotten in a single generation—have shown little inclination to get involved in a suicidal war. Yet in its foreign policy India still behaves like a highly vulnerable nation, though its only neighbors, besides Pakistan and China, are powerless Bangladesh and Burma. A golden opportunity to draw closer to the Pakistanis, who were looking eagerly for allies in the wake of the Russian invasion of Afghanistan, passed without action. Indians have pursued renewed Chinese relations on tiptoe, for fear of offending the Soviets as well as out of distrust of Chinese motives. Proposals for a "Himalayan defense," covering India, Pakistan, Bangladesh, Nepal, and Sri Lanka, have perished aborning. No longer can anyone deny India's utter dominance over these smaller nations, but this relationship of power awaits transformation into one of cooperation.

8

A Nation astride Past and Future

With over 700 million people scattered across a vast subcontinent, speaking 14 languages and 200 dialects, worshiping thousands of gods and practicing half a dozen religions, following the most varied styles in food, dance, and music, India wriggles out of the grasp of almost every generalization. Everything that can be said about it is true, but nothing is wholly true. Yet modern India is one nation and seems likely to remain so, and old India was, somehow, one culture, with a single social system, common values, a pervasive religion. So when we describe India we must take care not to weave its many strands into an overly tidy basket; at the same time we must see what all have in common.

We have looked at India from several points of view: its history, its religion, its politics, its development. If we sift all these together in search of a common theme or pattern, we recognize the picture of a nation simultaneously tugged by the past and the future. We should pause for a moment here to consider what it means for a nation to have a past. The United States has only three and a half centuries of history, and many of our ancestors arrived within the last 150 years. Like the first pilgrims they brought their own traditions, but more important, they brought their willingness to exchange old habits for new ones appropriate to their new home. Thus the American experience has been one of constant adjustment, experimentation, discovery. Americans escape their own past as the immigrants themselves did, moving from country to city to suburb, from east coast to west, from moral conservatism to permissiveness and perhaps, now, back to conservatism. The nations of Europe, with their thousand-year-old cultures, change more slowly. But Europe's two centuries of industrial progress have revolutionized almost every life, while three-quarters of a millenium of wars, migration, and tourism have brought people together, drawing them out of their own small world.

India's past, until recently, resembled an infinitely patient digestive process, working over the 3,500-year-old material of the Aryan arrival. Kingdoms rose and fell, the Khyber Pass echoed with the hoofbeats of one army or another, but life for most people presented few new conditions to adapt to; the Aryan system slowly refined itself, sinking its roots deeper and deeper into the land. Tradition became truth: whatever had been written in the scriptures, whatever had been practiced since time immemorial in daily life, could not be doubted. And to this innate respect for the past Hinduism added the belief that man's social life represented a cosmic plan, beyond question, beyond change.

Is it any wonder, then, that India names its telecommunications satellites after Hindu gods? Or that its gigantic conglomerates are still owned by the families who originated them—Tatas, Birlas, Kirloskars, Jains? The extended-family system may have outlived its usefulness in the world of big business, where companies are better run by professional managers and owned by stockholders, but the sophisticated, city-bred businessman can no more leave the family behind than the villager can walk away from the ancestral home. Young men and women in Bombay still permit their parents to choose a spouse for them, though now boys and girls mingle at school and elsewhere in a way that their ancestors would have found unthinkable. Educated professionals who consider themselves free-thinkers still join caste associations where they can mix with members of the same community. The caste, family, and marriage systems once served an essential function, but for many modern Indians this is no longer the case; yet Indians cling to these old forms because they offer a sense of security, the security of doing what has always been done.

In the villages, where things change more slowly, tradition rules with a far firmer grip and prevents people from adapting when circumstances change. New seeds and farming techniques may be available, but the peasant must see absolutely conclusive proof of their success before abandoning the old techniques. The washerman may not have enough customers to support himself, but he could no more think of trying another skill than of changing his skin. Untouchability has been illegal since the passage of the constitution, but for an Untouchable to stand on line with members of other castes remains a rare and possibly provocative act in most villages.

In politics the tokens of tradition remain crucial. Leaders like Jayaprakash Narayan and Vinoba Bhave, not to mention Gandhi himself, have owed much of their popularity to the image they conjured up of an uncorrupted India, strong in its simplicity. Political affairs have been marked by reform movements whose goals have lain somewhere in a perfect past. Earlier we mentioned the Arya Samaj, the nineteenth and early twentieth century movement for a purified Hinduism; the state of Maharashtra has been periodically shaken by the outburst of a cult revolving around Shivaji, a Maratha who cut the forces of Aurangzeb to ribbons three centuries ago. Even today it is dangerous for politicians to be seen in public there unless they are wearing the homespun cotton typical of the northern peasant.

India's process of development has remained strongly tied to the past. The relatively slow rate of growth owes much to India's reluctance to indulge in sudden change, such as large-scale industrialization or collectivized farming, as in China. The large subsidies doled out to cottage industries can be traced specifically to Gandhi, but they have remained popular because the idea of preserving native crafts in a world of mass production carries strong emotional appeal in India. Wealthier Indians rarely buy cottage crafts, preferring something more modern, but they would not like to see the industries vanish.

But the pull of the future, which India is approaching so warily, is powerful. The United States, with its highways and skyscrapers and factories and colossal, casual waste, exerts an almost mystical influence over the Indian imagination. It sometimes seems that half the college teachers in India are looking for fellowships to study in the United States; they want a trip to the future. On the slightest provocation Indians will denounce themselves for laziness, impromptitude, and, above all, superstition. Today politicians in the Gandhian mold are rapidly giving way to young men and women who promise to "get things done," as if efficiency were more important than the goals they want to accomplish. Indeed, much of Sanjay Gandhi's appeal resulted from the image of ruthless efficiency he projected, scheduling his meetings every three minutes, razing slums with battalions of bulldozers, disdaining conventions, rules, and customs. Sanjay, they used to say, "will get things done."

But India is part of the modern world in more than just its imagination. The mechanized farms of Punjab, the atomic research institute in Ahmedabad, the advertising firms comfortably quartered in Bombay skyscrapers—all are home-grown, not bought or borrowed from a more advanced nation, and they mark India's status as an advancing industrial nation, at least in part. Even the most obscure village has been touched by modern life in the form of electric lights, movies, radios, motorcycles, even wristwatches.

India's turmoil, then, is that of a nation clinging to an old identity while it inches toward a new one. Looking to its past with longing and looking ahead with trepidation, India finds itself astride two worlds, without a clear picture of what it wishes to be. There can be no turning back; India is like the villagers who finally leave for the big city and cannot return to the life they left behind. The process of change may seem slow to us, but we should judge India's modernization not by our own dynamic standards but by that country's own past. And in so doing, we can see that many of the conflicts we have described arise from abrupt change in a world that had previously been inert.

Communal violence, for example, clearly represents a struggle between an ironclad past and the burgeoning possibilities of the future. The landless and the zamindars are probably India's most tradition-bound classes, the one accustomed to submitting, the other to ruling. Both see a new world rapidly taking shape around them. The old landlords see their power being eroded, politically and economically, by the rise of a new class of aggressive, educated owners of medium-sized farms, the Jats. The low-caste tenants and the landless hear of villagers who have successfully established themselves in town, see new, fancy goods available at the village shop, and listen to the speeches of politicians on the radio, with their promises of freedom from poverty. Both sides place less faith in the ties that have bound them to one another over the centuries. So the landlords fear the future, while the poor peasants feel shut out from it. When the peasants begin to demand their rights, no matter how timidly, the old-fashioned landlords see the beginning of the end. With no one powerful enough to stop them, they launch their attack against the defenseless villagers. Thus they stave off the future and ensure that its eventual arrival will be a bloody one.

The problem that underlies all India's other problems is that of national unity—binding the country's hundreds of communities, each spinning on its own axis, into a single people, distinct in their many cultures but united in their sense of a common identity. The tug-of-war between past and future operates powerfully here. In the European nations centuries passed before the Normans, for example, came to think of themselves as fundamentally French, before the Galicians acknowledged that they were Spaniards. Among nations formed more recently the force of technology overwhelmed the force of tradition that makes people identify with their region or clan or religion, rather than their country. Italy was formed only in 1870, and Italians, who spoke a variety of dialects, continued to think of themselves as citizens of their old provinces. But the advent of radio, and "radio Italian"—Tuscan, the language of Florence—spread not only a single tongue but a sense of national identity. Sometimes people rebel against whatever national culture is being spread by modern technology, as the Iranians did by substituting the traditional religion for foreign ideals; but the rebellion proves the strength of the trend toward nationalism.

Indians have so many different traditional identities that the goal of a united people seems terribly distant. Indians align themselves with their religion, their caste, their region, their state; somewhere among these the country itself must fit. Indians hear themselves addressed on the radio as "fellow citizens," but they rarely speak of themselves this way. They won't even eat one another's foods, and they can't speak one another's languages. There can be no "radio Hindi," since All India Radio broadcasts in the various local languages. And deep loyalty to a religion does not coexist easily with deep patriotism. Karl Marx understood this and wrote that communism must serve as a replacement for state religion. India's traditional leaders, like Gandhi, have sought to use religious ideals as a rallying point for national fervor, but the result has probably been a strengthening of religious feeling at the expense of the secular state.

The existence of India's federal system acknowledges the country's unique problem with national identity. Only the fact that this system has been permitted to function has prevented the rise of secessionist movements, like those threatened during the language disputes of the early and mid-1960s. It may be no coincidence that the closest thing to a secession movement occurred in Assam during the prime ministership of Mrs. Gandhi, who continually threatened the independence of the states. It is the government in Delhi, after all, that is the new and suspect institution; the other sources of loyalty—caste, language, and region—have been around for a thousand years or more. It will be many years before an Indian is an Indian rather than a Sikh, a Jat, or a Punjabi.

Yet there can be no doubt that a government, or even a single leader, can do much to promote this sense of national identity. Josep Broz Tito, premier of Yugoslavia from World War II until his death in 1980, welded his national hodgepodge together by giving Yugoslavs a deep sense of national purpose and favoring no single group at the expense of others. China, the only nation that can be readily compared with India, required a bloody revolution, but it transformed itself from a land of warlords and independent provinces to a single country dedicated, with apparently profound discipline, to a common cause.

Perhaps the greatest tribute to Nehru is that, without resorting to violence or abridging the rights of states or minorities or non-Hindi speakers, he gave a strong push to the sense of national identity. As Tito was the ideal Yugoslav, so Nehru made himself the ideal Indian: passionate about his people but transcending all their divisions. Just before he died, he was still serving as a peacemaker between one group and another, but he had brought India a long way in the direction of nationalism.

Nehru's grandson, Prime Minister Rajiv Gandhi, has proved himself as free from the taint of religious and communal prejudice as his grandfather; he, too, is a truly national figure. The challenge that he faces is to continue the task of nation-building begun by Nehru, and continued, somewhat unevenly, by Indira Gandhi. He must gain the loyalty of all the people, bringing them together without threatening their diversity; so doing, he can help the old world to harmonize with the new and establish the nation that India has never been.

Facts about India

Population (1981)—685 million

Villages—550 million
Towns and cities—135 million

Hindu—560 million
Islam—82 million
Christian—19 million
Sikh—14 million

Population of principal cities:

Calcutta—9,194,000
Bombay—8,243,000
Delhi—5,729,000
Madras—4,289,000

Average life expectancy—52 years
Per capita income—$175 per year

158

Percentage of population below poverty line—46 (1978)
Literacy rate—34 percent
Railway passengers—3.9 billion per year
Principal crops—rice, wheat, sorghum, oilseeds
Principal languages—Hindi, Bengali, Marathi, Telugu, Urdu
Area—3,288,000 sq. km. (1,260,000 sq. mi.)
Population growth rate—1.9 percent

The twenty-one states of India:

Andhra Pradesh
Assam
Bihar
Gujarat
Haryana
Himachal Pradesh
Jammu and Kashmir
Karnataka
Kerala
Madhya Pradesh
Maharashtra
Manipur
Meghalaya
Nagaland
Orissa
Punjab
Rajasthan
Tamil Nadu
Tripura
Uttar Pradesh
West Bengal

Bibliography

Allan, John; Haig, T. Wolsey; and Dodwell, H. H. *The Cambridge Shorter History of India.* Delhi: S. Chand, 1964.

Basham, Arthur Llewelyn. *The Wonder That Was India.* New York: Taplinger, 1968. (A fine introduction to ancient India, generally available.)

Breman, Jan. *Patronage and Exploitation: Changing Agrarian Relations in South Gujarat, India.* Berkeley: University of California Press, 1974.

Burke, S. M. *Mainsprings of Indian and Pakistani Foreign Policies.* Minneapolis: University of Minnesota Press, 1974.

Chaudhuri, Nirad C. *The Continent of Circe: Being an Essay on the Peoples of India.* New York: Oxford University Press, 1966.

Chawla, Sudershan. *The Foreign Relations of India.* Encino, Calif.: Dickenson, 1976.

Cole, W. Owen, and Sambhi, Piara Singh. *The Sikhs: Their Religious Beliefs and Practices.* London: Routledge and Kegan Paul, 1978.

Constitutionalism in Asia: Asian Views of the American Influence. Berkeley: University of California Press, 1979.

Franda, Marcus K. *India's Rural Development: An Assessment of Alternatives.* Bloomington: Indiana University Press, 1979.

Frankel, Francine R. *India's Green Revolution: Economic Gains and Political Costs.* Princeton, N.J.: Princeton University Press, 1971.

Frankel, Francine R. *India's Political Economy, 1947–77: The Gradual Revolution.* Princeton, N.J.: Princeton University Press, 1978. (The best overview of modern political and economic development.)

Gandhi, Mohandas K. *An Autobiography: The Story of My Experiments with Truth.* Boston: Beacon Press, 1957.

Gandhi, Mohandas K. *Non-violent Resistance.* New York: Schocken Books, 1965.

Hutchins, Francis G. *India's Revolution: Gandhi and the Quit India Movement.* Cambridge, Mass.: Harvard University Press, 1973.

Kothari, Rajni. *Democratic Polity and Social Change in India: Crisis and Opportunities.* Bombay: Allied Publishers, 1976.

Lane-Poole, Stanley. *Medieval India under Mohammedan Rule.* Delhi: Universal Publications, 1963.

Lannoy, Richard. *The Speaking Tree: A Study of Indian Culture and Society.* New York: Oxford University Press, 1971.

Lewis, Oscar. *Village Life in Northern India: Studies in a Delhi Village.* New York: Vintage, 1965.

Masani, Zareer. *Indira Gandhi: A Biography.* New York: Crowell, 1976.

Mehta, Ved Parkash. *The New India.* New York: Penguin, 1978.

Mehta, Ved Parkash. *Portrait of India.* New York: Farrar, Straus & Giroux, 1970. (A highly literate and readable account of contemporary Indian life.)

Mellor, John W. *The New Economics of Growth: A Strategy for India and the Developing World.* Ithaca, N.Y.: Cornell University Press, 1976.

Naipaul, V. S. *India: A Wounded Civilization.* New York: Knopf, 1977.

Nehru, Jawaharlal. *The Discovery of India.* Garden City, N.Y.: Anchor Books, 1960. (A highly personal, nationalistic, and perceptive account of the great currents of Indian history.)

Pandey, Bishwa Nath. *The Break-up of British India.* New York: St. Martin's, 1969.

Tinker, Hugh. *India and Pakistan: A Political Analysis.* New York: Praeger, 1968.

Tyson, Geoffrey. *Nehru: The Years of Power.* New York: Praeger, 1966.

Weber, Max. *The Religion of India: The Sociology of Hinduism and Buddhism.* Glencoe, Ill.: Free Press, 1967.

Weiner, Myron. *Party-building in a New Nation: The Indian National Congress.* Chicago: University of Chicago Press, 1967.

Wiser, William H., and Wiser, Charlotte Viall. *Behind Mud Walls, 1930–1960.* Berkeley: University of California Press, 1963. (A pleasant, if slightly outdated, introduction to daily life in village India.)

Zimmer, Heinrich Robert. *Myths and Symbols in Indian Art and Civilization.* New York: Pantheon, 1946.

Index

A note on the author

JAMES TRAUB has lived and worked in India as a college teacher and as a journalist, traveling extensively throughout the country. At present he works as a freelance journalist. His articles have appeared in *The New York Times, Saturday Review, Barron's,* and other national magazines. He is the author of *The Billion Dollar Connection.*